DEMOGRAPHIC TARGETING

To Priscilla

Demographic Targeting
The essential role of population groups in retail marketing

JAMES A. POOLER
University of Saskatchewan, Canada

Routledge
Taylor & Francis Group

LONDON AND NEW YORK

First published 2002 by Ashgate Publishing

Reissued 2018 by Routledge
2 Park Square, Milton Park, Abingdon, Oxon OX14 4RN
711 Third Avenue, New York, NY 10017, USA

Routledge is an imprint of the Taylor & Francis Group, an informa business

Publisher's Note
The publisher has gone to great lengths to ensure the quality of this reprint but points out that some imperfections in the original copies may be apparent.

Disclaimer
The publisher has made every effort to trace copyright holders and welcomes correspondence from those they have been unable to contact.

A Library of Congress record exists under LC control number: 2002019583

ISBN 13: 978-1-138-73935-2 (hbk)
ISBN 13: 978-1-138-73931-4 (pbk)
ISBN 13: 978-1-315-18416-6 (ebk)

Contents

List of Figures

Chapter 1

Demographics and Shopping: Introduction

A harried, middle-aged female shopper hurries into a clothing store in a mall. She is on her way home from work, needs a new outfit for Friday night, and has to get home to cook supper before she takes the kids to their evening soccer game. She is desperate to buy something and wants to purchase it quickly and efficiently. She does not want to walk all over the mall, nor does she want to drive all over town looking for clothes. She just does not have the time.

At the same time, in the same store, there is a teen shopper. She is on her way home from school and is in no hurry. She has nowhere to go, has all the time in the world, and is not really anxious to make a purchase right away. She is just looking around. She will probably wander the mall for a couple of hours and maybe she will shop more on the weekend with her friends.

Simultaneously, a husband on his way home from work enters the same store. He is looking for a gift for his wife. He hopes to find a good selection in this one store. He is not inclined to visit a number of different stores because the whole experience makes him uncomfortable. He just wants to find a nice sweater, with a minimum of fuss. Price is really no object as long as he can just find a nice item to buy and be on his way.

What we see at work in these three situations is the important role of demographics in retailing. We have three people shopping in the same store but because they belong to different demographic groups, they take entirely different approaches towards their shopping goals. In addition to different objectives, they also have different budgets and their shopping schedules and patterns are completely dissimilar. These three shoppers provide a good example of the critical role that demography plays in shopping.

This book studies the impact of demographic groups on shopping. As it undertakes this task it pays special attention to the roles that sex, and especially age, play in patterns of shopping. The book is organized around the theme of demographic groups – each chapter identifies a group and then takes a look at the likely shopping patterns for that group. We can refine our ability to sell to shoppers by targeting the demographic groups to which they belong. This exercise is called DT – demographic targeting – and is designed to give us the greatest potential insights into the shopping patterns of consumers. Demographic targeting plays an essential role in reaching retail markets.

We can say a lot about people and their shopping behavior simply by examining their demographic group membership. For example, *middle-aged shoppers have less time available for shopping but more money.* Such ideas provide valuable information about how we should sell goods to them. It says we should sell them items that are convenient and easy to buy, and it says that they are probably willing to pay a premium price to get such products. It also says they may be looking for a bundle of items under one roof. Similarly, we can say that *teen shoppers have a lot of time available for shopping but less money.* Such information provides a clue as to how to market products to teens. It says we should sell them items that are inexpensive. It says they have lots of free time to find what they want – they will comparison shop. They will take their time shopping and they may look at an item several times before they buy it. My teenage son is a perfect example of this style of shopping. It tells the retailer to be prepared for finicky but determined shoppers. It also tells the retailer that his prices must be aggressive for teens because they will be very aware of the competition's prices.

The retailer who ignores the demographics of his customer does so at his peril. As the examples above demonstrate, having knowledge of the demographic group to which customers belong tells us a great deal about their needs and desires as shoppers. Demographic targeting is the key to success for modern retailing.

The modern shopper can best be understood by considering him or her to be a member of a distinct demographic group that has shopping needs that are particular to it. This book takes a look at shopping from the perspective of demography and considers the demographic group to be a crucial concept for understanding the modern shopper.

What are the Demographic Groups?

Turn on the radio. What do you hear? Does it seem to you that no matter where you turn the dial you hear songs from the sixties? If so, you are not alone. The fact of the matter is that there is a good reason why songs from the past dominate the radio dial. The reason is found in demographics. The biggest and best-known demographic group, and the one that most people have heard about, are the baby boomers. This is that large group of children that were born in the years following World War II, mainly from about

1946 to 1964. People were happy and optimistic about the future after the war, and so birth rates soared to new heights. The result was the birth of the baby boomers, that group of people that are now between forty and sixty years of age. This is a massive group of people and throughout their lifetime they have come to dominate virtually everything they touch. Why are there so many songs from the sixties on the radio? Because the boomers are a big market and this is thought to be the music they prefer to hear.

The boomers dominance of the radio is a good example of a demographic influence that affects everyone. Wherever you go, whatever you do, you hear music from another era. Drive in your car, go to a restaurant, walk through a store and you are likely to hear music from the past. The boomers were teenagers in the sixties and their musical legacy continues to dominate the airwaves just as they themselves dominate the marketplace.

There are other well-known demographic groups. Many people will have heard of Generation X, the supposed lost generation that lives in the eclipse of the early baby boomers. This group of people, later born boomers, is said to suffer the consequences of living in the shadow of the early boomers. For instance, it is said that the early boomers took all of the best jobs before Generation X could get to them. Another well-known demographic group is found in so-called Generation Y that is considered to consist of the children of the baby boomers. The idea is that the big group of baby boomers all had their children at about the same time in life and this caused another mini-boom in the birth rate. Generation Y is considered to be a demographic group that is overindulged and spoiled by its wealthy parents, and one that was raised on Nintendo and MTV. Generation Y has never seen inflation or war and as far as they are concerned, the stock market always goes up. They are said by some to live in an unrealistic world because they have lived highly protected, affluent lives.

These three are the best-known demographic groups. The idea of classifying millions of people into convenient groups is a popular one. It lets us simplify the world and talk about it as if it consists of just a few simple groups. This book takes this idea but broadens it and puts it to use in the study of shopping. It says that not all shoppers are alike but that we can distinguish between them based on their demographic groups. It says that *all* shoppers can be classified into unique shopping categories and that it is easier to understand shoppers by looking at them as members of a demographic group.

By understanding demographic groups, we can better understand how people will shop and what they will buy. Knowing that a shopper is male and fifty years of age tells us something important about him. If he is a busy executive at mid-career, it tells us that he is primarily interested in buying high-end items that will bolster his self-esteem and pay himself for the hard work he does. On the other hand, if a shopper is sixteen-years old and female that tells us that she is probably interested primarily in clothing, make-up and fashion. The basics of age and sex tell us a great deal about shoppers, and how they will shop. They also tell us a great deal about how retailers should market their products and how advertisers should approach their audiences. Demography is important.

The New Shopping

At the same time that there is a new significance to demography, there is also a new shopper out there. Whether she is middle-aged or a teenager, she is shopping at a different level of needs than her ancestors. While people once bought goods for which they had a real physical need, the new shopper shops on a higher plane. She is shopping for reasons – emotional, psychological – that are totally different from those of the past. This book is also about retailing in this new world. It is impossible to appreciate the significance of demographics without reference to this new world of shopping.

The retailer must get in step with the new shopper. He must tune-in to the new shopper and come to realize that she is shopping at a different emotional state than her sisters of the past. No longer is it sufficient to try to appease the modern shopper with old-fashioned goods that offer quality and value. The new shopper wants possessions that satisfy her soul. She is shopping for goods that fulfill her need for personal self-actualization – for inner well-being and emotional contentment.

There was an important psychologist in the 1940s who revolutionized the way we think about ourselves. Abraham Maslow invented a new way to look at how people live their lives; how they order their priorities and set their very goals in life. Maslow suggested that life consists of five levels. The five levels range from an elementary one where we satisfy the most basic needs – like those for food and shelter – to one where we satisfy our highest psychological needs – like those for inner emotional fulfillment. Maslow suggested that the higher needs can only be fulfilled once the lower needs are met. This book argues that when it comes to shopping, our lower level needs *have* been met and that we are now shopping on a higher plane, where a higher level of needs is being satisfied.

This book is also about why we shop. It says that we shop to self-actualize – to fulfill the highest level of Maslow's Hierarchy of Needs. It says that the modern shopper can only be understood if he is viewed as a being that is shopping to fulfill high level, emotional needs. It says that the modern retailer can only survive if she *targets* herself to this new kind of shopper. Demographic groups must be viewed from the perspective of this revolutionary change in the very nature of shopping.

Getting basic consumer needs is now a trivial matter for most people. Everyday items are readily available and almost everyone has enough income to take care of the fundamental essentials of food and shelter. We are living in an affluent society. As the basic levels of Maslow's set of needs are more easily met, consumers move to a higher plane. We have moved beyond the basic levels into those where emotion and personality come into play. We used to be happy to have a nice house and a clean car. Today our feelings of inner well-being, achievement and prosperity arise from a more intricate world. Today we feel good when we wear fashionable clothes, drive a sophisticated vehicle, or own the right designer labels. There has been a change in priorities, and retailers need to grasp that the consumer's mind is on a different level than it used to be. Whether it is the young adult demographic, or the baby boomer group, the importance of this new mindset is crucial to understanding the modern shopper.

Shoppers used to be content to buy a simple cup of coffee. Today they demand a double grande latte from *Starbucks*. The everyday simple shopping experience of buying a cup of coffee has been replaced by one where the customer gets an emotional lift and a sensory experience from the event. This simple example is truly indicative of the way in which the new shopper is evolving to a higher plane of needs. What other products can duplicate the success of *Starbucks*? How else can everyday products be elevated to the point where they provide an almost therapeutic experience?

Whether it is for a $2 cup of coffee, or whether it is for a $50,000 vehicle, today's shopper shops for the mind. The shopper who buys an expensive sport utility vehicle is just like the shopper who buys at *Starbucks*. He is not just buying transportation. He is buying self-confidence, self-esteem and a boost for his ego. He is buying an emotional lift, he is making himself feel good, and he is probably rewarding himself for the good job he does at work. The purchase is about everything *but* transportation. The purchaser of the sport UV is buying an image of himself and his lifestyle. It is supposed to say that he is a rugged, off-road type of person who likes the great outdoors and who likes to get away from it all. Today's buyer of a sport UV is shopping at a higher level of needs than the shopper of the past. It is all about psyche and emotion.

The *Starbucks* example and the sport UV example provide good indicators of the true nature of the modern shopper. There is a revolution underway in the way we shop. From our obsession with designer labels, to our fascination with buying for emotional reasons, there are profound changes taking place in shopping. This book examines shopping from the ground up and with an eye towards the idea that shopping today is on a higher level of emotional need than ever before. This is true for all demographic groups. There is a new world of shopping out there that does not work by the old rules.

Shopping the Levels

One way to look at the mentality of shopping is to suggest that it consists of a number of levels, just like Maslow's Hierarchy. On the way to shopping at the highest state there exist other levels of shopping needs. There are five levels that Maslow identifies and these are illustrated, in the form of shopping levels, in Figure 1.1. At the bottom is a level of shopping for basic physical survival needs. This includes shopping for necessary foodstuffs and other essentials of existence such as shelter and basic clothing. This is the shopping that people must do to survive. It is shopping that is usually routine and habitual – shopping for basic groceries or other household essentials.

Figure 1.1 A Shopping Hierarchy of Needs

At the second level there is shopping for security needs. In Maslow's Hierarchy it is argued that people have a basic need for personal security. In shopping this comes about through purchases of items for health and safety. Everyday necessities such as toiletries are part of this kind of shopping, as are purchases of medical or dental services. Similarly, shopping for items related to personal hygiene is part of the second level of shopping.

Shopping at the first and second levels does not overly engage the senses. It is traditional shopping, as we know it. At this level, shopping is a practical affair and shoppers are not really shopping for the mind or for emotional reasons. This is shopping for everyday basics and as such it often involves filling the food cupboard. Shopping at this level can involve any product so long as the shopping experience is seen to be routine by the shopper. Buying that gift for Uncle John, buying a new washing machine, or even buying a car, can be a dull, uninspired and even painful event for many shoppers. The essence of distinguishing between the different levels of shopping is often found not in the goods that are being bought but in the emotional investment of the shopper. For example, buying that gift can be excruciating for some people. Alternatively, buying a gift for a loved one can create a sense of joy and emotional uplift for others. The levels of shopping are not so much in the goods being bought, as they are in the minds of the shoppers.

In spite of the apparent routine of shopping at the first and second levels, shoppers do engage in shopping for value and so this kind of shopping can be challenging. Comparing products, shopping for good prices and looking for bargains become the order of the day. This kind of shopping can be demanding and rewarding, and many people put in a serious effort in shopping for good deals. Nevertheless, this kind of shopping is not meant to be mentally stimulating or emotionally rewarding. It is mostly about getting the job done where such shopping is viewed as a routine matter of survival.

At the third level of shopping comes shopping for belonging and social acceptance. As we shall see later, this kind of shopping plays an important role in the purchases that people make. Every demographic group, from children to adults, has a need to feel social acceptance and the feeling of belonging, usually to a group of some kind. The group may be informal (a circle of friends) or formal (a church). In either case, studies show that the sense of belongingness that is created by group identity is crucial to human psychological well-being. Shopping for belongingness includes behaviors such as teens buying the 'correct' clothing to fit in with friends or adults buying the 'appropriate' sporting goods – such as golf clubs – in order to establish membership in an informal social group. Shopping to belong is a central part of a great deal of shopping behavior and we shall see how it plays a role for almost all demographic groups.

At the fourth level of Maslow's Hierarchy comes the need for personal self-esteem. This includes the need for self-respect, the respect of others and for prestige. When it comes to shopping this involves buying possessions that 'make' the person in the eyes of others. Owning and buying particular products can make one feel good and can create feelings of self-esteem. An adult might create feelings of self-worth by buying a particular new vehicle that provides a sense of personal well-being and raises the self-image. A teen might achieve similar goals by buying new clothing that is the latest in style. In either case, just owning a product is essential to creating a sense of feeling good about oneself. Many of the items that people buy, they buy for reasons of self-esteem.

Finally, at the fifth level comes the shopping for self-actualization. This is where many shoppers are shopping nowadays and as we shall see this is the level at which retailers and advertisers should be directing their efforts. This is shopping for the self, shopping to define the self and shopping for self-fulfillment, personal growth and personal happiness. This is what modern shopping is all about. Shopping at the fifth level is undeniably the essence of today's shopping behavior.

Shopping at the fifth level is a type of shopping that can be readily exploited by retailers and vendors. It has very little to do with acquiring the basic necessities of life, as does shopping at the first and second levels. Neither is it about building self-esteem or belongingness. Rather shopping at the fifth level is about shopping for the self as a form of inner fulfillment. As such it is about buying things that have little or no relation to practical necessity or physical need. Instead it is about buying items *for the soul*, for the inner-self as a form of self-reward, and for the pleasures of shopping itself. Retailers and advertisers should be aware that many shoppers are functioning on this higher plane, where price and practicality have little or nothing to do with a purchase. Self-actualizing shoppers are willing to buy whatever it takes to satisfy their inner needs for self-fulfillment, and are anxious to achieve a sense of accomplishment and personal growth through their purchases.

Shopping for Time

A housewife used to take great care in shopping for, and preparing her meals. Today she orders her groceries over the Internet and makes a meal from pre-processed foods that require a minimum of preparation and cooking. What is her reward for this? In the time she saves, she signs up for a craft class in which she is able to express her artistic desires. She spends extra money on the groceries to free up extra time for herself. A husband used to take great care in washing the car by hand in the driveway. Today he runs the car through the car wash so that he has time to make it to the investment club meeting that he attends. He spends extra money to make extra time for himself. Both of these consumers are changing their shopping patterns so that they have more time for higher order pursuits.

People are shifting to higher order needs in all aspects of their lives. They hire housecleaning services to free up time for other activities, rather than spend their time vacuuming. They buy pre-packaged, prepared foods because they have better things to do than peel carrots. They hire professional services to cut their grass because they want to spend more time on the golf course. They go to a clothing store that offers a complete wardrobe service because they do not have the time or the inclination to go all over town looking for clothes. In short, people are looking to shift their activities from the mundane tasks of yesteryear to those that allow them to perform at a higher order. Maslow was right. He just did not see how people would come to direct their purchases and their shopping behavior toward self-actualization.

The Purpose of this Book

Shoppers can best be understood by looking at their demographics and by targeting them according to their group membership. Demographic targeting is crucial for understanding shoppers and for marketing to them. This is not a revolutionary new idea in marketing, but one that needs to be defined and restated in a modern context. Demographic targeting is the key to success when it comes to understanding shoppers.

This book will appeal to retailers, marketers, advertisers, sales people, manufacturers, designers and anyone who is connected to the retail trade in some manner. It will also be of interest to shoppers and casual readers who are interested in the psychological and emotional aspects of everyday shopping behavior.

By looking at shoppers according to their age and sex we can try to get a better grip on the nature of the retail market. Each of the chapters that follow examines a specific demographic group in the context of the modern era of shopping. The discussion ranges all the way from infants and toddlers right up to the aging baby boom demographic. What we shall see is that every demographic group is important to the retail market and that every group is unique. It is only by looking at the retail marketplace from the perspective offered by demographics that we can gain a true understanding of modern retailing and marketing.

Chapter 2

The Young Parenting and Infant Demographic: Time-Pressed

Picture this. A grandmother is searching for a new baby outfit for her first-born granddaughter. She is fussy about what she wants and she spends many hours looking for that perfect outfit. It has to be just right. Not only has she got a lot of time to spend shopping for this item but also price is really not an important consideration. It is more important to her to get a cute outfit than it is to worry about a few extra dollars.

Now picture this. The young mother of that same granddaughter is taking a brief break from her demanding schedule at home. She has taken her daughter out shopping with her, but she knows she only has a couple of precious hours until it is feeding and naptime again. She needs to buy formula and diapers but also wants to promptly pick up a couple of outfits because her daughter is growing out of her old ones. On this mother's budget getting a good price is crucial. The young mother simply wants to pick up one or two practical outfits, while she shops for other items, and get back home as quickly as possible.

What we see at work here is the important role of demographics in retailing. We have two people shopping for the same product, but because they belong to a different demographic group, they take entirely different approaches towards their goal. In addition to different objectives, they also have different budgets and their shopping schedules and patterns are completely dissimilar. This example is a good illustration, not only of the complexity of the retail market for infants, but also of the different needs of shoppers that belong to different demographic groups.

One would think that infants would make up one of the most insignificant retail demographics of them all. After all, their shopping needs do not seem very great and they certainly do not go out shopping on their own. Nevertheless, in spite of their size, infants form a substantial portion of the retail market and they have the shopping clout to make themselves a meaningful part of the retail demographic. Infants are not themselves shoppers but they are very important to the adults around them. As a consequence, adults – mothers, fathers, friends and relatives – shop avidly for this group. As the example above illustrates, different demographic groups have very different shopping motivations when it comes to this group.

The infant demographic is a multi-faceted one. There is the casual shopping of older relatives, there is the hectic shopping of the parents and, as we shall see, there is also more important and directed shopping undertaken by the parents. Unravelling the retail threads of the infant retail demographic is intriguing.

The Basic Necessities of the Parenting Demographic

Convenience is the watchword for the young parenting demographic. Infants place huge demands on their young parents in terms of time and effort. As a consequence, the young parenting demographic will be looking for services or products that efficiently save time and improve their ability to satisfy their children's needs. The young parenting demographic is a busy one. Between infant care, career demands, and the daily demands of everyday life, young parents have little time to spare and little time to waste. They are shopping for time.

There is a long history of improvements to the quality and efficiency of infant products and this serves to illustrate how the parenting demographic has driven the market over the years. Steady gains have been made in the ease that parents have with products. A good example is found in the invention of pre-packaged baby food. Long ago parents had to strain grown-up food by hand for their infants. This was a difficult and time-consuming process, but all it took was a simple insight to see a way around it. According to the *Gerber* website, it all started in 1927 in the kitchen of Daniel and Dorothy Gerber:

> Following the advice of a pediatrician, Dorothy Gerber had been hand-straining solid food for her seven-month-old daughter, Sally. After many evenings of repeating this chore, Mrs. Gerber suggested that her husband try it. After watching him make several attempts, she pointed out that the work could be easily done at the Fremont Canning Company, where the Gerber family produced a line of canned fruits and vegetables. Daniel Gerber, covered in strained peas, thought his wife had a good point.

Dorothy Gerber's insight led ultimately to the development of the *Gerber* line of strained baby foods. Nearly 190 *Gerber* products are now distributed all over the world. The huge commercial success of the invention of baby food demonstrates that it filled a gap for a need that existed. It is an exemplary example of the creation of a product that made life easier for the young parenting demographic. Many other such products exist. Canned formula and disposable diapers are two excellent examples of successful products driven by parenting demands. The market was there for these products because they added convenience and efficiency to young parent's lives. The young parenting demographic wants products that make life simpler and the market often responds with items that fulfill this goal.

Reusable, stick-on-tabs have replaced old-fashioned pins on diapers, disposable wipes have replaced washable cloths, snaps have replaced buttons, and Velcro has replaced laces. A steady stream of products and inventions has made life easier for this young demographic. This is a demographic group that is intolerant of products that waste time or effort; their goal is to satisfy their children's needs with as little fuss as possible. The market has responded well to the needs of this group and will undoubtedly continue to do so. Innovative new products that produce efficiencies for parents are limited only by the creativity of those who identify new product niches for this important group.

The bulk of the retail requirements for infants consist of everyday basic necessities like formula, disposable diapers, and baby food. The availability of these basic products will drive most of the shopping behavior of the young parenting demographic. The young couple will tend to shop for those basic necessities wherever it is easiest for them to do so. Since grocery and large department stores are readily available in most places, and usually offer good prices, they will probably be the frequent source for acquiring most of the basics of infant life.

The pattern of shopping for infant necessities has very important consequences for the retailer. It suggests that much of the shopping that young couples carry out will be of the *one-stop* variety. It implies that when a young mother goes shopping for an infant requirement, such as diapers, it is also important to make available to her all of the other products that cater to the baby market. Items such as strollers, car seats, playpens and especially toys and clothing should be available wherever diapers, baby food and formula are sold. The busy young couple does not always have the time to go driving around searching for all of the other products that they require. It only makes sense that retailers should target the young parenting couple as a shopping unit that wants one-stop access to many infant needs. This is particularly true when one takes into account the extra inconvenience that couples face when it comes to transporting young infants from place to place.

The busy twenty-five-year old couple with a couple of young children is also shopping for good price. The one-stop convenience of shopping needs to be combined with excellent value and good selection. The retailer that can satisfy all of these needs simultaneously will be the one that wins the shopping dollar of young parents. They want value priced merchandise and they want it all conveniently located in a single location. The wise retailer offers a *bundle* of infant related products that satisfies virtually all the needs of young parents. Many of the big merchandisers like *Wal-Mart* already take this approach to infant retailing. The young parenting demographic is one of the most time-pressed groups of all, and anything that can simplify their lives – in the same way as baby food or disposable diapers – is bound to be a success.

We also know that seventy-five percent of all shopping is done by women, so it follows that the majority of shopping for infant necessities will be undertaken by the mother. This will be especially true in those situations where the mother of the young infant is staying at home for at least a portion of the infant months and so supposedly has more of an opportunity to go shopping for basic necessities than does the working husband. This means that the one-stop shopping center for infants should especially target its marketing efforts to the busy young mother. This is the woman who tends to be doing her shopping on a tight schedule most of the time. And, it is probably safe to say, that the young female shopper is often on a fairly tight schedule regardless of whether she has the kids in tow, or whether they are staying at home with Dad while she shops.

Brand names are important when it come to infant necessities. *Gerber*, discussed above, is just one good example of a well-known name that parents appreciate and trust when it comes to meeting their children's needs. There are many other such names in the baby business – *Pampers*, *Playtex*, and *Heinz* to name just a few – that have gained a well-earned reputation for quality and reliability.

The grocery store is the most likely location for the one-stop infant shopping center. There is a simple reason for this. It is a place that the young parenting demographic will visit, regardless of infant needs. Since there is likely to occur a weekly or biweekly trip to the grocery store anyway, why not make it the place where most infant needs can also be met. While many grocery retailers sell the basic supplies of formula, diapers, and baby food, as well as a basic line of baby clothing, they fail to offer many of the other basic items that young parents will be likely to buy. If a grocery store has a fruit and vegetable department, and a meat department, so too should it have an infant needs department.

The Significance of High Quality in Baby Equipment

Over and above the basic necessities of food, formula and diapers there exists a huge world of retail demand for equipment related to young children. For the young parenting demographic this represents an interesting stage of life. There are a whole host of baby products that are needed in the infant years. These specialized products are only needed once in a lifetime, during the childbearing years, and once that time has passed these products are relegated to a garage sale. Yet to the young parent these products, although fleeting, are very important. In fact, more than anything this is a time in life when the *quality* of products becomes very meaningful.

There is a great deal of specialized baby equipment that young parents need including strollers, playpens, cribs, bathinets, bassinets, high chairs, booster seats, change tables, car seats, and so on. When they shop for such items, this demographic has a certain level of expectation regarding quality. This is not seen as a time to shop for second rate, bargain products. When it comes to their children, people shop for the best, and usually they are seeking out a product they can trust to be safe and reliable. This often means that young parents shop for products with well-known brand names. There are many companies that have gone to great lengths to establish credible brand name identity in the child care area, and theirs are, by-and-large, the products that are trusted by young parents.

For retailers it is imperative, not only that they stock well-known, high reputation products but also that they back it up with impeccable service. It is also important to note that the price of baby equipment, while important, is probably secondary to quality. Young parents will shop for value, but only among those products that are perceived to hold a high level of quality.

A good example of a well-known product line that has earned the respect of generations of young parents is the *Fisher-Price* group of products. These products are exemplary of high quality and earned respect, and they are trusted and well-liked by parents. This is in spite of the fact that premium prices are usually charged for these products. They demonstrate clearly that the young parenting demographic is willing to pay a higher price for reputation and quality. This message should not be lost on retailers and manufacturers. Parents want to take care of their shopping needs and be highly efficient at it, but they also want to buy the best for their kids. They want to ensure that everything in their lives is of the highest quality. Nothing can be second rate when it comes to their children.

Making Time for Parents

There is room in the parenting market for still more products that save time and simplify childcare. One important idea is to look toward products that *create time* for young parents. An excellent example of this phenomenon is found in the widespread and common use of baby monitors. While these are often thought of as being devices that are directed towards the security and personal safety of infants, they should also be considered as important devices for the *time* that they create for young parents. The baby monitor, in effect, lets the parents be in two places at once. This affords them the ability to do other activities while they watch the baby. While these activities may be as simple as cooking, cleaning or watching television, the monitors also allow many productive parents the opportunity to work at home. Thus baby monitors do not just increase the time available for other basic household activities; they can also be very important devices in regard to the economic productivity of the household in the modern childcare setting.

There is a challenge in this for manufacturers and retailers. What other products or services can be used to provide more free time for the young parenting demographic? In the old days, diaper services were one such popular service that made life simpler for young parents. While these still exist, they have been largely made obsolete by the existence of disposable diapers. But what are the other services that have yet to be invented? What can be done, in other words, to increase the free time that parents have available to them? Clearly the baby monitor is one of the most important inventions in the history of childcare. The goal of duplicating its success presents a real challenge to manufacturers, retailers and service providers.

An interesting development in the area of providing time for young parents comes from the *Unilever Company* (makers of *Dove* and *Lipton*) that announced it was going to expand into the business of offering services to clean homes and do the laundry. This is another marketing idea that is appropriate to the times, as people of all ages struggle to find enough hours in the day. Although there may be many young couples who cannot afford such cleaning services, there are also many more with young children who will be more than ready to hire such a service. Some mothers and grandmothers may scoff at the idea of a young mother hiring a service to clean her house – after all, they managed to do it themselves. But there are many young couples with busy and active careers that just do not have the time to handle basic household cleaning chores *and spend time with the children.* When it comes to a choice, many young parents will opt for the cleaning service. It frees up the extra time that can be invested more wisely in attending to the more important nurturing chores that fall to them. In the long run, the extra money may be well spent. After all, what is the point of having a career if one does not use the profits from that career to invest in things that make life better? Most parents would agree that having a well-adjusted infant is much more important than having a spotless house.

If major companies are going to go into the business of house cleaning, why not consider the idea of professional babysitting services? The bane of every young couple's existence is finding a trustworthy and reliable babysitting service. This should be a large area of demand in the years to come. More women are working and there is a greater demand for babysitting than there ever has been before. There are two broad areas of babysitting demand. There is the situation where people typically hire a teenager to watch a child for a few hours in the evening while they go out. But much more importantly there is demand for infant care during the day when parents are at work. Many people are uncomfortable with the idea of daycare for very young infants and would prefer to have a babysitting service where the attention is one-on-one, at home, and individual.

It is surprising that companies with well-known and trusted names in infant care have not launched babysitting services of both types. Would it not be reassuring, for example, to be able to call a bonded, insured, reputable and entirely trustworthy babysitting agency out of the yellow pages when you need a babysitter? One can imagine such agencies hiring older, experienced women to serve as in-home or drop-in babysitters. Although it may be difficult to compete with teenage babysitters on price, one suspects that many people would be willing to pay a premium hourly rate to get a babysitting service from a well-known company they can trust.

One of the most valuable things in our modern world is time and, more and more, people are willing to pay top dollar to free up quality time. A major, brand name babysitting service would be enormously successful in being able to sell the luxury of worry-free time to young parents. They need only follow the lead of the housecleaning services that have earned themselves a reputation over the years of being trustworthy. Any business can be successful if it carefully builds a good reputation and this idea applies to childcare as well as to any other in-home service.

Stress Reducers

In addition to providing the young parenting demographic with extra time for other activities, manufacturers and retailers can also target their efforts towards creating services or products that remove stress from young parent's childrearing years. An excellent example of this process at work is the recent introduction to the market of disposable training pants. Gone are the days of trying to teach toilet training by having the child go without diapers. These innovative new training pants represent a combination of a diaper and a pair of pants. This allows toddlers to go 'without diapers' while having the security of absorbent pants. Not only does this product make life simpler from the practical perspective of doing laundry, it also takes a great deal of stress out of the lives of toddlers and parents alike. The pressure and anxiety of toilet training have been greatly relieved by this simple product. No longer are parents overly concerned about hurrying-up the toilet training process – the pull-up training pants allow the event to proceed at its own pace. In fact, the media report that the average age for completion of toilet training is actually on the rise as young parents stop trying so hard to accomplish the task at an early age. For parents, gone are the pressures of the cost of wasting extra diapers during training. For infants, gone are the stresses of having accidents with regular clothing. This is a brilliant marketing idea whose time was long overdue. It makes one wonder how many other such products are just waiting to be invented.

Some market watchers insist that all of the big products have already been invented and that there is really nothing new that can be created. The recent success of disposable training pants proves just how wrong this theory is. There are undoubtedly other products that have yet to be developed that can reduce the stresses of raising children. The young parenting demographic can use all of the help it can get in making life easier. The best source for such ideas is to be found in identifying the *problems* that parents have, and then inventing products or services that solve those problems.

New technologies are just waiting to be exploited in the area of childcare and, as a new example shows, these can be used as a stress reducer. The Internet, in combination with video cameras, can be used to let parents at work visually drop in on their children at daycare. Through a desktop Internet connection parents are able to see their children whenever they feel like it simply by looking in on video cameras that are installed at daycare centres. Thus the parent at work can actually see their child throughout the day with the reassurance that everything is all right. This not only relieves stress but eases the guilty conscience of the working parent who must otherwise spend the entire day without seeing their child. This is another excellent example of a big stress reliever for the young parenting demographic, and one that probably not only makes them happier and more self-assured, but also makes them more productive employees. It is a good example of another idea whose time has come, and one that employers should be anxious to provide. This is a strategy that will keep and attract high quality, young employees. Moreover, it is another good example of a big stress reliever for the young parenting demographic.

Store and Cart Design

There is nothing quite like the sight of a young mother with a couple of infant children in tow as she makes her way into a grocery or department store. A typical pattern is to see a young Mom with an infant car seat/carrier use two shopping carts, one for the infant car seat and another for the items she wants to buy. She pushes one cart and pulls the other, all the while juggling infant care with shopping decisions. Even more impressive is the mother who does this while she simultaneously looks after a couple of additional children, one in the shopping cart seat and another toddling along. Such shopping expeditions are quite a feat and even the most confident men would be wary of attempting such difficult manoeuvring of temperamental children and uncooperative shopping carts.

What do store and shopping cart designers do for such women? Is there any attempt to design products to make life simpler or easier for the busy young family when it comes to shopping? There is a whole area of product design where the needs of particular shoppers have been overlooked. Take the basic shopping cart, for example. New products, such as infant carriers have evolved over the years, yet shopping cart design has remained basically unchanged for fifty years. How many stores go out of their way to cater to the young parenting demographic when it comes to shopping cart design? If they did, they might find that they would draw in a larger portion of this important shopping demographic.

Shopping carts are standard across the land. Few attempts have been made to redesign the shopping cart for a new era. One of the most ingenious inventions of all time was the idea of building a child seat into the standard shopping cart. It was brilliant. It contains the child, it puts him facing the mother, it keeps him secure and it puts him at eye level, and within easy reach. Moreover, when the seat is not needed it can be folded away so the cart can be used by anyone, with or without child. Outstanding idea. People have come to expect this feature wherever they shop and the person who first thought of the built-in child seat in the shopping cart should be acknowledged as a true genius.

Store design and layout also leaves much to be desired. Pity the poor man or woman who attempts to go shopping in a major grocery or department store with a stroller. Typically the store aisles are under designed for strollers, being too narrow to accommodate their needs.

Parents have trouble manoeuvring through them and other shoppers have trouble getting around them. Recently a major chain announced that it was opening an experimental store with wider aisles specifically designed to accommodate strollers. The young parenting demographic will tend not to patronise those stores that do not go out of their way to accommodate them. How often, for example, have you noticed that a store will have extra wide aisles in the vicinity of the diapers, formula and baby food?

How Parents Shop to Define Their Children's Sexual Identity

Given the emphasis on practical and everyday products in the sections above, the reader may come to believe that these are really the only products of concern to the young parenting demographic. Nothing could be farther from the truth. In fact we have not even yet touched upon the most important retail area of them all when it comes to this group. There is another whole area where marketing should direct itself and in reality, this may be the one true area of real guaranteed *growth* for this demographic.

Aside from the practical aspects of the products discussed above, there is a completely opposite force at work in the lives of young parents. Because, while they want to be *efficient,* they also want to be *effective* as parents. This presents an interesting challenge to both parent and retailer alike. The fact of the matter is that a very large part of the shopping that parents do is directed towards defining their children's sexual identity. While most marketers direct their thoughts and efforts to satisfying the *obvious physical needs* of the young parenting demographic, there is a much more important psychological aspect to the shopping behavior of young parents. Understanding this psychology is a crucial element of any marketing strategy for this group.

The first and most obvious way in which the young parenting demographic starts to define their children's sex is through color. Almost every parent starts to buy pink or blue clothing for the young infant. It is patently clear from this behavior that it is important to a young couple to start defining their children's sex even when they are just weeks or months old. In fact, this starts even at only a few days of age. And it makes a difference. How people will react to and respond to a baby is in no uncertain terms determined by the sex of the baby. And the parents, who want the sex to be clear to other people, go to great lengths to ensure that the color of dress is appropriate to the sex. Young parents do not like it when strangers mistakenly identify their child as being of the opposite sex. The fact that an infant girl has not yet grown enough hair to be recognised as a girl by strangers is upsetting to young parents. They want the sex to be correctly recognised and they do not want strangers calling their girl a boy. As a consequence, when they shop for their infant son or daughter they buy blue or pink so as to convey a strong message about the sex of the child. For manufacturers and retailers there is a clue here. Young parents want products of all kinds that demonstrate the sexual identity of their child. Diapers, for example, for very practical reasons, come in versions for boys and for girls. But what if infant seats or strollers were to be labelled as being more appropriate for one sex or the other? Would parents buy them? Certainly they would, just as certainly as they buy bicycles that are designed especially for boys or for girls.

The message is that manufacturers and retailers cannot go too far out of the way to sell products that are associated with the sex of children. Parents are very conscious of the sexual identity of their children and this demographic usually welcomes any product that will reinforce this idea.

The point is further reinforced by the extent to which hairstyles are considered to be important by young parents. This behavior is demonstrated quite readily by the fact that parents of girls will let their hair grow long as soon as possible, while parents of boys will cut their hair as soon as it starts to grow. The purpose of this conduct is to ensure that the sex of the baby is clear to all observers. Just like the pink and blue clothing, this common behavior among young parents provides a ready clue as to their concern with this subject. Products for infants that help to identify their sex are likely to outsell others in the marketplace.

How Parents Shop to Define Their Children

There is much more at stake however than the issue of sexual identity when it comes to shopping for infants. Parents not only strive to define the sex of their children through their shopping, they also try to define them as human beings. For example, even when it comes to simple items like sleepers for infants, parents often have a choice between a variety of designs. Very often these designs will have *themes* associated with them. For example, there are sleepers with a sports theme, sleepers with an education theme or sleepers with a music theme. Through their purchases of such items, parents are starting to define their children's personalities and their behavior. This is *shopping to define the self* and it forms a central and important part of all shopping behavior.

What message are young parents trying to convey? What does it say when they dress their child in clothing with a sports theme? Some would say it is just cute. But there is more to it than that. Such parents are trying to send a message – to themselves, to the child and to any and all observers – about how they see their child and about how they aspire to his future. Why does a parent choose a sports theme over an educational theme? Does this behavior send a message to the world about how they see priorities in their child's life, and about what is really important to them? Sure it does. It is the parent's way of defining the child. Costuming is very important in defining the persona and young parents demonstrate by their behavior that they are anxious to start to define their children's personalities as soon as possible in life.

The essence of this discussion is to point out to retailers that the young parenting demographic is shopping for a lot more than is immediately obvious. The young couple walking through the store may be shopping on a much higher plane than is directly evident. When we get beyond the basic necessities of childhood, young parents are literally shopping their *hopes and dreams* when it comes to their children.

Although we have discussed just clothing to this point, it is clear that toys form another large part of the process of shopping for self-definition. The father that buys his infant son a ball glove or the mother that buys her daughter a cooking set sends a strong message about aspirations in life. Parents express their deepest desires for their children through the articles they buy, even though most of those articles may be, on the surface, just toys. Retailers should be aware that the young couple shopping for infant products might be shopping in a mode that is intended to define and shape the very personality of their child. This suggests that there is a lot of room in the market – in fact, this may be where most future growth will occur – for providing products that serve no practical purpose other than to define the self.

Is self-definition the *real* purpose of toys? Consider an example. Compare the parent who buys their infant stacking rings – an educational toy – to the parent who buys a miniature football – a sports related toy. Are such toys really for the benefit of the child or do they actually serve the needs of the parent?

Is there room in the market for products that simply help parents to define their children as people? How many extra sleepers can be sold if they are marketed as products that are intended primarily to sell a theme to parents? Consider the other products – cribs, playpens, car seats and so on – that could be marketed, not only with the sexes in mind, but also with various lifestyle themes as a central feature.

In addition to clothing and toys there are many other possibilities for shopping parents to define their children. Consider room decorations and furniture, towels and bedding, or bottles and dishes. All of these products, and many others, present the possibility for parents to further define their children. While many such theme products already exist, the point to be made is this is possibly a real growth area for many infant products. While many products carry designs and decorations that are cute, there may be a whole new world of demand out there for products that simply define the persona of the infant. Parents are probably far more concerned about this aspect of infant care than many entrepreneurs imagine. Shopping for child-defining products becomes more than an exercise in wishful thinking on the part of the parents. It also makes a clear statement about how the infant is seen in the eyes of the parents.

Designer Label Babies

Another interesting aspect of the way that people shop for their infants is found in the type and style of clothing they will buy. While many parents will try to economise and shop for infant clothing at discount department stores, there are also many parents who are anxious to have designer label babies. These are the parents that buy designer label clothing, even for very young infants. An interesting question from the retailing point of view is to ask what it is that such parents are trying to accomplish? What is the purpose of the designer label baby?

Many people would answer that the young infant dressed in designer label clothing is simply cute. There is nothing quite like an infant dressed up to look like a grown-up. But is that all there is to it? Probably not. Many parents go out of their way to buy nothing but designer label clothes for infant children. What are they trying to accomplish? The answer is that they are dressing the child in a way as to show off their own fashion acumen. This style of dress has little or nothing to do with the child and everything to do with the parent. This is the parent's way of showing off, of demonstrating fashion awareness and an ability to keep up with the times. This is the parent dressing the child as a miniature version of themselves – as a so called mini-me – in the hope of demonstrating their own fashion sense. Designer label clothing on infants sends a message to other adults about the extent to which the fashionable parents are in style. It is an extension of the self – it is dressing the children for one's own self-definition – rather than dressing for the children themselves.

Retailers, advertisers and manufacturers should be aware that there is an enormous market for designer label infant clothes. This is a strong fashion trend that is likely to get stronger in the future. The extra cost of such clothing does not act as a deterrent to the determined parent shopper. There is a very high level of demand for infant sized designer label wear and in most cases the premium price seems to be well worth it to the shopping parents. We saw above, that when it comes to their children, most parents want nothing but the best. This idea speaks volumes about the likelihood of there being a continuing strong demand for upscale clothing for infants.

Advertisers and retailers should also be well aware that by dressing their children in designer label clothes parents are also, by extension, dressing themselves. This has important implications for the ways in which children's clothing, and especially children's designer label clothing, are marketed. It is not about making your children look good, it is about making yourself look good.

Infants – Two Worlds of Retail

This chapter began with an example of the different approaches to shopping taken by young parents as opposed to grandparents and relatives. This distinction is an important one in the retail market for infants. In particular it can be said that there are *two* distinct markets for children's products. It follows from the discussion in this chapter that, on the one hand, there is a *practical* market for infant and child products. Young parents especially will be on a tight budget and will be looking for good value and good price. This is the sensible side of purchases for young children. But there is also another entirely different market for children's items and apparel. It can be called the *extravagant* market. This is the market for friends, relatives, grandparents, and sometimes even parents, where price is often no object and where quality, style, and fashion are the bottom line when it comes to shopping. The latter market is typical of the designer label products discussed above.

There are clearly two sets of shoppers out there for infant needs, especially clothing, and there are two distinct markets to be served. What is the retailer to make of this split demographic? The answer is clearly that while some retailers will try to market to both halves of the infant demographic, others will find it more appropriate to target one half or the other. One retailer may wish to offer only upscale, designer label infant wear at a premium price. Another will be tempted to sell good quality but everyday products at a discount price. In spite of the distinction between the two groups, the bottom line is that all shoppers shopping for infant wear probably want to be able to buy both types of products simultaneously.

Most shoppers, parents included, will be tempted to buy both discount products for everyday use, as well as high end products for showing off. The smart retailer will make both types of product lines available to the market at the same time. There is really nothing contradictory at all about young parents buying discount priced sleepers and at the same time buying expensive designer label pants. Similarly, the shopping relative or grandmother may well be interested in purchasing several high-end, expensive products together with budget priced everyday wear.

Infants are just like adults. They have more expensive, high-end clothing for when they go out and mingle, and they also have more practical, everyday clothing for around the house. Parents 'dress-up' their children when they take them out. It is not only a way of showing them off, but it is also a way of making a statement about themselves as parents. Style is important. Just like adults who dress up for the office, or for social occasions, infants are expected to be dressed according to circumstance. The psychological message that dress and clothing are important is conveyed from a very early age.

The fashion industry has done such a good job of promoting its products that even infants can be dressed in style. This is quite an accomplishment. Parents and relatives are prepared to pay any price to make sure that infants are fashionable. The reason for this is that the style of dress of those infants conveys a message to the world about their adult parents and it is through their efforts in dressing their children that they define themselves as parents. The young parenting demographic is important in more ways than one, and advertisers and retailers should regard infant wear as a serious business.

Chapter 3

Young Children:
The End of the Age of Innocence

At a *very* young age children usually do not have any particular selfish desires or wishes about what they wear, how they look, where they go, or what they do. We are talking here, of course, about very young children; say in the two to six-year age group. This is the so-called Age of Innocence.

For the most part, it is left to the parents to buy things for very young children and to make their choices for them. In turn, young parents are concerned primarily with defining their young children's lives. By the items they buy, the clothes they wear, and the activities they participate in, parents hope to be able to mold and direct the course that their children will follow as they start to grow up. Parents usually have very definitive ideas about what their young children should become, and they start at a very early age to buy for them the things that will make them turn out as desired. Retailers should be very aware of these subtle aspects of parenthood and should be prepared to offer the young parenting demographic the particular merchandise it desires.

The classic example of this sort of behavior is the young father who buys his two-year old son a ball glove. Although it will be several years before the son is ready to use the glove, the father is so anxious to start to direct his son's life that he buys it anyway. Such behavior is usually treated in a lighthearted and almost comical way by the rest of society. It is seen as amusing that the father is so eager to help his son start to grow up. Unfortunately, such behavior is really serious business. Parents have specific goals for their children and they are eager to start them on the road toward those goals.

Life-Defining Clothing

Parents try to define their children through the clothing they buy. As was indicated in the previous chapter, this trend starts in infancy with the traditional distinction between blue and pink clothing. Thus, even when infants are just a few hours old, the adults around them start to define them as people. This trend continues throughout infancy and early childhood as parents dress their children according to their goals for them. Such purchases will determine how other adults respond to and interact with infants and young children. If a young boy is wearing a shirt with a baseball theme, the shirt will play a role in how other adults and relatives see and talk to the child. At a very early age, certain expectations are created. He knows even at two years of age, for example, that the men in his life, such as grandpa, expect him to play baseball. This is important. It happens to all children at all young ages. It determines the course of their life and expresses hopes for them. Parents set the boundaries of this behavior by the clothing they buy for children and no one should underestimate the potential power of such messaging.

These ideas set important challenges for the retail and manufacturing sectors. For infant and children's clothing, messaging is a very important criterion. One can cater to the young parenting demographic by stocking clothing and accessories that play to their emotions as concerned parents. One might imagine, for example, that more clothing should be available that convey a definite theme or message. Sports, education, music, dance, the arts, and other such themes should be popular sellers with young parents who are concerned with making a statement through their children's clothing. The designers of children's clothing that insist on using neutral themes are losing a large market. Parents will be more likely to buy products that convey a specific message to the world about their child.

One might also think that when it comes to buying clothing for young children that parents are concerned primarily with finding good value at a good price. In fact, it would seem that it has been a tradition for decades that parents will shop for high quality, durable items that stand up to the rough and tumble play of young children. While these goals still remain in effect to some extent, it is also possible to state that shopping for young children has undergone a revolution in recent years. Parents are now less concerned with substance and quality and are more concerned with style and fashion. How they dress their children says something about them, and more than ever parents are concerned about making the right fashion statement.

The ages between two and six used to be thought of as the Age of Innocence. It was a time in life when children were free of the pressures of style, fashion and conformity. It does not last long anymore. It used to be that children were unconcerned and ambivalent about style. Kids dressed like kids and were indifferent to the social pressure to conform. But over the last thirty or forty years the powers of the fashion industry have relentlessly and unabashedly forced their way into the lives of children. Fashion and style have become all the rage, and even children as young as five and six years old have begun to feel social pressure to conform to clothing norms.

Girls in grades one and two will want to dress and look like their latest rock star idols. The influence of the *Spice Girls* in the 90s was a strong example of this phenomenon. In an effort to sell more products, the fashion industry is constantly pushing the boundaries of the Age of Innocence, making it more important for even young children to feel pressure to dress according to trends. While adults will often think that it is 'cute' that youngsters want to dress as grown-ups, this trend is far more important. It shows that the fashion industry has succeeded in extending its reach into the youngest age groups, and shows no mercy in the extent to which it makes its presence felt. The idea that a young child of six, eight or ten years of age is free to dress as she wants, and is able to enjoy the innocence of youth, is long since past. At that age it is now more important to 'look cool' and to dress and behave like one's peers.

The remaining time of childhood innocence has been reduced to the youngest ages of all, but even very young children are being dressed in the latest fashions *by their parents*. Truly, the Age of Innocence has been all but vanquished by the fashion industry in its relentless quest to gain an ever-larger share of the market. The business of children's clothing and dress must now be considered as prime territory for the fashion world, regardless of the age of the children. Retailers should be aware that even for the youngest children, the Age of Innocence is on the wane.

There is a warning in this trend for retailers. There are some chains, such as *Wal-Mart*, that do not stock well-known fashion labels. The direction in the industry indicates that this is a practice that is not likely to succeed in the future. The efforts of the designer label industry to make its presence felt have been successful, regardless of the age of the shopper. This suggests that, even for clothing for very young children, designer labels are a necessary feature. Retailers who insist on going it alone may find that they are left behind when it comes to clothing sales. Some retailers respond to this trend by creating their own lines of so-called designer label clothing, but as shoppers get more sophisticated, even the youngest ones will demand the latest well-known 'real' designer brands.

The trend towards an obsession with designer labels is evidenced by the existence of chains of stores that cater exclusively to the high-end, children's market. *Gap Kids* and *Baby Gap* are good examples of the extent to which retail has turned itself toward exclusively servicing the children's market. The fact that such chains exist at all, speaks volumes about the huge market that exists for the young parenting demographic. It is important to parents that their children be in style and dressed in the latest designer labels. There is definitely a new mode of shopping for this demographic that is substantially different from the days when their parents simply shopped for low price and good value in children's clothing.

Grown-ups define themselves through the things they buy. Clothes, cars, houses, and other items help to define the person. The same is true of infant and child clothing. Parents define their own lives through the things they buy for children. When it comes to selling products and services to the young child demographic, the primary target is really to be found in their parents. This is a significant idea for entrepreneurs. It says the young parenting demographic is mostly concerned about defining itself through its purchases for children. It says that children's clothing should be designed with adults in mind and that neutral clothing is likely to be less successful than clothing that conveys a life-defining or fashion message.

There are other areas in which there is a high-end obsession with getting the right look for children. Hair styling, for example, is one area where parents expect more than they used to. While a basic, no-nonsense haircut would have sufficed years ago, people now count on getting their youngsters hair styled when it is cut, and even colored. Hair stylists would be wise to appreciate that the hairstyle is really for the adult, rather than the child, and to pitch their product accordingly. It is important to parents that their children have the right look, especially when it comes to showing them off to others. Hairstyle is an important part of the equation.

Another similar area where there is an adult emphasis on the look of children is when it comes to jewelry and, especially, pierced ears. It is very common nowadays to see parents having their children's ears pierced at a very young age, even at a few months, and it has become a common trend to see this practice among boys as well as girls. Parents just cannot wait to see their children dressed up as young adults and it seems there is no age where it is too soon to start to do so. To parents, an infant girl with jewelry is just like a girl in pink; it is an attempt to start to define her as a person and as a young lady. Retailers of such products should bear in mind that, from the parent's point of view, it is never too early to use shopping as means of self-definition, for both parent and child.

Life-Defining Entertainment

Have you ever gone to the circus, *Ice Capades*, or other children's entertainment and noticed that some parents bring children to the events that are far too young to understand them? You know the ones. They will bring an infant to the circus in the hope that the child somehow appreciates what she is seeing. This is a good example of a trend among parents. At the earliest age possible, parents are ready to buy their children life-defining experiences. Sometimes they are so enthusiastic they buy such experiences even when their children are unable to comprehend them. Nevertheless, nothing is too good for their children and age is seen as no barrier to the introduction of important experiences.

This is the retail world of entertainment for children. Most parents are obsessed about buying experiences for their children and no retailer should underestimate the extent to which young parents are willing to spend money to acquire them. The young parenting demographic is concerned with trying to define their children and buying entertainment experiences is seen to be an important part of this endeavor. In the simplest cases, parents will buy admissions to local events like circuses or entertainment shows. In more extreme cases, parents will buy major destination trip packages, even for toddlers. In either case, the goal is to bring to one's children what are seen to be important experiences that will shape them as people and will enable them to become well-rounded individuals.

Retailers of children's entertainment should be primarily aware that parents are not buying entertainment. Rather, from their point of view, they are buying life-defining experiences that will influence their children's very development. This is important business. Mickey Mouse is not just entertaining to the children; he is part of a well-rounded child development program. Parents think it is important for their children's growth for them to experience as many things as possible when they are young. A trip to Disney World is an *investment in experience* – it is not just entertainment.

Marketers of children's entertainment should be aware that the parents are primarily interested in buying an educational experience for their children. The entertainment value of the product is secondary to the learning experience that it provides. Marketing children's entertainment is not marketing entertainment at all; it is marketing what is seen to be a learning experience to young parents.

For advertisers there is also a strong element of 'keeping up with the Joneses' when it comes to kids entertainment. Retailers of these products could market the competitive aspects of their packages. People are very sensitive to these issues and they can be easily exploited by appealing to their sense of keeping their own children's experiences on par with those of their friends. Parents are extremely competitive when it comes to their children and no marketer should underestimate the strength of these compulsions when it comes to selling entertainment products to the young parenting demographic.

A good indicator of the competitive drive that parents experience comes from the movie business. The continuing success of children's movies pays homage to the great significance that people place on their children's experiences. Next to teen hits and general audience blockbusters, children's movies are among the most successful of them all. Why? What is it that drives parents to take their very young children to the latest *Disney* movie? Once again the answer is that parents see themselves as providing their children with more than simple entertainment. They see such movies as part of the developmental experience of a well-rounded child and they are willing to go to any lengths to acquire these experiences. For example, this is again an entertainment industry where we see parents taking children that are far too young to appreciate or understand what they are seeing to movies. But in their zealousness to give their children the best of everything, parents will take even young, confused toddlers to the latest blockbuster children's movie. From the parents point of view they cannot wait to give their kids the best of everything.

Marketers and advertisers of children's movies should appreciate that parents are not just buying an afternoon's worth of entertainment. Far from it. Instead they see themselves as buying a developmental experience for their child that is essential to his or her psychological and emotional well-being. This is vital to parents. Seeing the latest hit movie is part of creating a well-adjusted, successful child. When a child's movie is marketed to an adult it is important to emphasize these motivations.

Room Decorating

A big area of interest among the young parenting generation is found in the business of decorating children's rooms. As was the case with clothing and entertainment, there is more at stake here than meets the eye. There is a concern once again to attempt to define a child and to direct his life through the way in which the room is decorated. Parents will choose a theme for room decorating, such as sports or music, and this is another part of their subconscious attempt to direct the course of the child's life. For retailers there is a huge source of business here just waiting to be exploited. Parents would be far more willing to decorate rooms for young children with a 'message' if it were just easier to do so. As it stands, there are very few retailers that cater in a deliberate way to this special type of demand for products in theme decorating, yet it is an area of potentially large sales.

Shoppers have moved beyond the world of just buying goods that meet their basic needs. Years ago, for example, it was adequate to furnish a child's room with basic items of furniture and a minimum of decorations. Today's self-actualizing shopper is looking to satisfy *emotional* needs when she shops and will not be satisfied with old goods and services of the past. When today's shopper shops for room decorations she is shopping to fulfill her own psychological needs and desires. She wants items that allow her to express her emotions and feelings about her child, and she wants items that convey a message to the world about her hopes and dreams for the child.

When it comes to room decorating for children, major stores should have a department that is devoted to this very need. *Wal-Mart, Home Depot* and others should be prepared to sell theme room decorating items in bundles, with a maximum of convenience to the consumer. This department should have themed beds and furniture, matching curtains and wallpaper, and coordinating carpeting. There should be tables, chairs, lamps, change tables, cribs, and dressers that are conducive to the theme. There should also be ceiling fans, wastebaskets, blinds, light fixtures, pictures, knick-knacks and other related items. In addition, sheets, bedding and pillows should be coordinated as well. This is the kind of department that the modern parent wants to shop within – one that meets her demands for life-defining, children's decorating. It is a department that would be a huge success among parents and one that would draw out demand for a line of products that is just waiting to be exploited. As has been said before, when it comes to their children, there are not many things that parents will not buy. Their children's lives are their number one concern and there is pent-up demand for products that are seen to help to define a young child's life.

The themed room is, of course, for the parents. The actual decorations will have little if any effect on the child. But that is not what matters. What is important is that the parents feel a sense of accomplishment and achievement through their efforts. This is what it is all about. Perhaps the parents feel guilty about leaving the child in daycare during the day. The elaborately themed room will ease their guilt and make them feel that they are better parents. If their child has to go to daycare by day, at least at night he returns to a room that is all his own and one that reflects a steady and loving lifestyle. This is shopping at a level that goes beyond the acquisition of everyday goods – it is shopping that is about satisfying the emotional needs of the parent shopper.

Toys and Creativity

Is there anyone happier than an adult in a toy store? Is this not a shared, common experience that is enjoyed by all adults? Sure toys are for kids, *but who buys them?* Toys are for kids, but *toy stores* are for adults. Retailers and manufacturers alike should realize that their products, although designed for children, are purchased by adults and so a very important component of children's products is found in how adults respond and react to them on the shelf. If one were going to study toys for retail purposes it would be better to spend one's money on the study of the adult shopping experience rather than the play experience of the child.

What are toys? They are a part of play, a very important activity in the life of a child. Children have a lot of time. Unlike adults, who are always scrambling to fit enough activities into a day, young children have all the time in the world. In fact, it is easy to say that filling those hours of free time is one of the biggest jobs that parents have. This is where toys come in. They are essentially the primary equipment that is used to fill the many hours of free time that young children have. The question is, then, how can retailers, manufacturers and advertisers supply the best products to fill this large and important segment of consumer demand? In answering this question, it is important to emphasize that this is also one of the most unusual areas of consumer demand because we have adults buying things that they are not going to use for themselves but that they take great joy in buying.

The over-riding concern with the design of a toy is in the extent to which it catches a child's attention and thus becomes useful in occupying the child. Presumably a toy that holds a child's attention also has value in regard to creativity and imagination, otherwise why would it so occupy the child. This is the kind of toy that shopping parents prefer to buy. It is important to them that the toy has properties that stimulate the child's mind and inventiveness, and also that it is seen to aid in the child's development.

What goes through the parent's mind when they choose a toy? Color, quality, price, stimulus value, creativity and other such factors must all simultaneously swirl through the shopper's mind. This is a very complex decision; in fact it is probably one of the most complicated shopping decisions of all. There is a strong air of intuition and passion input into the decision to buy a toy, and it is one at which parents spend a lot of time and emotional energy.

What is important? Clearly what is considered to be one of the foremost variables of significance is color. Check through any recent line of children's products and what you will see is that a multitude of bright colors appears to be a crucial factor. The emphasis on color is definitely focused on the parent shopper and all parents assume that bright colors are important when it comes to children's products. This provides a strong clue to manufacturers and retailers; it shows quite clearly that product design and promotion should focus squarely on the parents. It is only their judgment of what is important that really matters in the shopping decision.

How does one convey an air of creativity or stimulation with the design of a toy? This is a very subjective area and one that is open to the whims of the parents. Retailers would do best to insist in their product labeling that a child's product promises creativity and development. People tend to believe what they read, so if a product promises in writing to be stimulating, the shopper is probably more inclined to buy it.

What about quality and value? Here it is necessary to repeat once again that, when it comes to their children, parents set their standards very high. They will only want merchandise that is perceived or reputed to be of very good quality. They will be willing to pay extra to ensure that they get the highest quality. Many manufacturers have already come to realize that perceived quality is more important than price with children's products. Some companies, like *Fisher-Price*, are able to charge premium prices for what are perceived to be top quality, reliable and trustworthy children's products. There are many manufacturers of children's products that have gone out of their way to ensure a solid reputation. This is a critical factor when it comes to children's items.

What else sells parents on products? Certainly an important element with toys is nostalgia. People like to buy toys that are traditional or those having a long history. A *Raggedy-Ann* doll is a good example of a product that people will buy because it has a historical sense to it. This is an important cue for retailers. It demonstrates again quite clearly that parents shop *for themselves* when it comes to buying toys. Another similar trend is for people to buy their children the same toys that they themselves had as children. Thus products like *Winnie-the-Pooh* continue to have strong sales because shopping parents like the tradition that is associated with the product. Such products may have no qualities that make them better as toys; parents simply buy them according to their own personal experiences.

Much like clothing, entertainment and room decorating, toys are also intended to be life-defining. People will buy toys that have a sport connotation, or those that are educational, in the hope that they will play a role in shaping personality, intelligence and life-style. When parents select toys they have a whole world of ulterior motives in mind. These are not just toys; they are hopes and dreams for the child's future. Retailers should sell parents the things that will satisfy their fantasies about their children's lives. Advertisers should approach the parent as if he or she is shopping in an illusionary world of hopes and expectations and one where the sky is the limit as far as the parents are concerned.

Parents buy sexist toys. Traditional sexist stereotyping continues to be a strong factor with the young child demographic and parents and relatives alike participate in the ritual. Toys send very strong messages to children.

Parents love buying toys. In fact, this shopping experience is one of the bonuses and rewards of having children. It is one of the most interesting of shopping experiences, yet it is also one of the most difficult. Many different factors come into play in the toy shopping experience and retailers would be best advised to keep in mind that they are really selling these products to people who are at heart still children. They shop by emotion, and by instinct, and the wise retailer will appeal to their inner child when he markets his wares.

A favorite strategy of retailers when it comes to toys is to use a toy to sell another product. The classic and best-known example of this approach is found in the snack *Crackerjacks* that has long included a toy as part of the product packaging. Not to be outdone, cereal manufacturers have for many years also tried to boost sales of their products by including a toy or a prize inside the box. These are outstanding examples of dual marketing strategies of using one product to sell another. Today, one marketer who has used this strategy in a highly effective manner has been *McDonald's* restaurants. In fact, most young children now see the primary purpose of a visit to *McDonald's* as getting a toy, where the food is simply seen as secondary. The success of *McDonald's* sends a strong message about the effectiveness of this approach as a marketing tactic.

Television

Parents need to fill their children's hours of free time with entertainment and activity. Since the 1950s a new player in this endeavor has been television. So useful is it in occupying children's time that it is sometimes referred to as an electronic babysitter. Although it does not seem like television is 'purchased' like other bought items, the truth of the matter is that when people choose to turn on the television they also thereby choose to turn on the advertisements that come with it. So in this way, television is an item that is consumed just like any other. Similarly when we browse channels, we are literally 'shopping' for the entertainment that we most prefer. Think of it this way. When you just walk around a department store and look at the merchandise, are you 'shopping'? Most people would say that, yes, they are. Browsing the ads on television is much the same experience.

When it comes to television for children, what do people shop for? The answer is high quality. People are shopping for children's television programming that is at a higher level than in the past. Many years ago children's television shows were presented as pure entertainment, with little or no deliberate educational input. Some readers will remember shows like *Howdy Doody* that were focused purely on fun and amusement. In later years, things changed. Parents started to demand higher quality programming that contained intentional educational material. Children's shows like *Sesame Street* led the way for such programming and set the standards to which many other new shows now aspire.

The truth of the matter is that when it comes to using television as a babysitter, parents want better content. They are shopping at a higher level. It is no longer adequate to just fill children's time with mindless babble; parents demand, and receive, television programming that is at a higher level of sophistication than its predecessors. This is another instance of the way in which people have moved to a higher level on the hierarchy of needs. Parents insist that today's shows not only be educational but also that they teach values such as caring and sharing, and principles such as honesty and fair play. Parents have come to expect a lot from children's programming and this is a good indicator of the higher plane of needs upon which they are functioning. Television for young children has come to be a medium that parents expect to be nurturing and enriching and not just one that aimlessly fills the hours with bland entertainment.

Television is important. It helps to define and create children. Studies show that children, even very young ones, spend many hours in front of the television set. More importantly, children spend many hours watching commercials. Although there is a lot of children's programming that is commercial free, there is still a large amount of programming that is laden with advertisements and even at a very young age children start to be inundated with product endorsements. To the producers of such television, creating demand for products is the bottom line. Shows that best hold children's attention are the ones that dominate the airwaves because they are the ones that will be the most successful in promoting products. Nevertheless, advertisers should be aware that parents today are more demanding and are shopping at a new level of sophistication. There is plenty of room in the market for quality children's television shows that offer programming that appeals to parents who are looking for something better. The new parent wants television form and content that is conducive to child development and well-being.

Daycare

This book argues that modern shopping is taking place at a higher level of need than used to be the case. Nowhere is this truer than with respect to daycare for children. Although we usually do not think of child-care as a form of shopping, it most certainly is. Parents pay for daycare as a method of *buying time* for other activities, usually work. It is a product that people purchase for themselves, in the same way that they buy time by having a yard service. The time that is purchased is usually put to a higher use. Although this is often work related, it is very regularly also directed to other activities such as shopping or recreation. In many households, for example, part-time daycare is pursued so that mothers or fathers might have time for a trip to the mall, or an aerobics class. Daycare is a commodity just like any other that is purchased to create extra time.

Daycare is big business. A report from the Bureau of Labor Statistics estimates that in 1998 about 65 percent of women with children under six years of age were part of the labor force, compared with only 44 percent in 1975. According to the Urban Institute's 1990 national child care survey, about 5.8 million children under the age of five are in child-care facilities.

How do people shop for daycare? While trustworthiness and reliability are key ingredients, cost is also an important factor. Retailers of daycare services strike a fine balance between the quality and reputation of their service, and the ability to provide it at a low cost. While there are some parents who can afford to pay top-dollar for daycare services, most of them are concerned with getting a good price. It is an important investment for parents, as they trust their most prized possession, their children, to strangers.

An important idea in the context of daycare services is the one that says a stay-at-home mother gives up potential income by staying at home. In other words, the mother who stays at home could be out working and so is giving up that income that she would otherwise make. When a working mother chooses to use daycare services she is usually able to offset the cost of the daycare by the income she makes while working. Daycare only makes economic sense if the income earned is higher than the cost of the daycare. In some cases, however, women choose to work even when the cost of the daycare exceeds the job income. They have career reasons for doing so.

Buying daycare is a relatively modern phenomenon. Years ago, tradition had it that mothers stayed home while men went to work. Now for social and economic reasons, women are choosing more than ever before to re-enter the workforce after childbirth and to employ daycare services to make this possible. This is a good indicator of the fact that society in general is shopping at a higher level than it used to. As more women stay in the workforce, they purchase the time required to do so, through daycare. As was suggested in the preceding chapter, it is surprising that more big-name businesses have not gotten into the business of providing daycare. While this is an area that is still dominated by small entrepreneurs and local businesses one can expect that in the future this retail area will come to be dominated by big business. It is just too lucrative for them to ignore.

Big Families – Children to Define the Self

One of the most important reasons why people shop is to define themselves. Modern shoppers buy things to make a statement, to show off their personality or to boost their own self-esteem. It follows that the very act of having children is also an act of self-definition. People have children to make their life more fulfilling, to round their existence, or to raise their own level of pride and self-respect. Having children is as much about boosting the ego, as is shopping. It is about acquiring a possession, a child, and about how that possession redefines ones life.

Children are something to display, like purchased items. People preen them, dress them up and 'decorate' them when they take them out. They like to show them off in the same way that they do a new car or a new house. A new child is something of which to be proud and the new 'owners' of such children wear them proudly. More importantly from the perspective of this book is that children become a medium through which to exhibit purchased items. Clothes, shoes, toys and accessories are all part of the child's image, and parents like to create that image through the things they buy.

People are able to demonstrate their resources through the *number* of children they have. A large number of children is now a status symbol, a demonstration of affluence and success. Years ago, tradition was that poorer people had larger numbers of children and a large family was indicative of a lack of family planning. A big family was seen to be characteristic of poverty, or indifference toward birth control. Today this situation is reversing itself. A big family is now becoming a status symbol, an indicator of prestige and prosperity.

The magic number is four. While having three children goes beyond the societal norm of two, four sends a message that the large family is deliberate, planned for and, most importantly, affordable. Having a large family makes a statement that the family can afford not only the basic necessities such as food and shelter, but also often implies that a family is wealthy enough that the mother (or father) is able to stay home full-time. The latter message is the most dominant one that the big family conveys. It says, 'We can afford to have one partner stay home and watch the kids'.

Having the affluence to have a large family is a status symbol and many successful couples demonstrate their success by having a large number of children. It is important to remember that the stay-at-home spouse is able not only to stay at home but to forego the income of the job they might otherwise have. It is a true statement of wealth.

What does the large, four-child family imply for shopping? First of all, it says that the couple can afford to own a house that is big enough for a family of six. It says that a five or six bedroom house is not only necessary, but is within the financial means of the household. It also says that the family can afford the vehicles that are big enough to transport the group. The big van or the extended sport UV becomes standard equipment for such a family. Perhaps more than one vehicle is required. The large family also says that food and clothing for four children is well within their means. Parents of two children will appreciate the extra costs that would accrue if the number of children were to double. In sum, a large number of children imply that a family is prepared to shop more and to buy more of everything, whether it is sports equipment or bedroom furniture. Retailers should be aware that the trend towards having larger families, as a status symbol, is a social phenomenon that is on the upswing. It will be increasingly important to market products toward this growing and affluent group.

The large family is also usually indicative of a situation where it is within the means of the family to afford to pay for services that buy time. Very often the family that can afford four children can typically also afford nanny services, housecleaning services, and so on. This suggests a growing market for services that buy time for the large family, including daycare and child sitting services. There is more wealth than ever before within society and much of it will be spent on the services that buy time for the wealthy.

Chapter 4

Pre-Teens:
The Shopping Pressures of Growing Up

These are difficult times for pre-teens. The forces of the global fashion industry have reached right into our households and have literally stolen the innocence of childhood from our youngsters. Children as young as five and six years of age are pressured by their friends to wear the correct fashions. Children in grades one and two are ostracized by their peers if they do not conform to the latest styles in clothing. The innocence of childhood has been lost to the international forces of capitalism, which has made 'consumers' out of even the youngest children. The world has changed, and with it the retail environment has undergone a transformation in recent years.

Pre-Teens and Fashion Pressure

When did it all start? When did pre-teens become obsessed with fashion and style? If we think back fifty or sixty years we can imagine a time when teenagers emulated their movie heroes and tried to dress like the celebrities they admired. Later, these trends continued with television. How much of a role did Dick Clark's *American Bandstand* play in the evolution of teen fashion, for example? Throughout the sixties, seventies, eighties and nineties, young people tried to dress and act like media stars and, at the same time, followed fashion trends among their peers. Over this period of time however there has been a relentless downward pressure on the age at which it becomes appropriate to do so. While it was once just teenagers that were slaves to fashion, it is now common for younger kids to feel the same. Over the years, both manufacturers and retailers have become aware that a younger and younger market could be readily exploited. The process has evolved now to its logical conclusion. While it was once just teenagers that were driven to distraction by fashion demands, it has become commonplace for all children to suffer from fashion pressure.

It is not fair. Kids used to be free to wear a shirt and jeans, and to just be kids. Now there is pressure to conform – to be 'cool' – and accordingly to act less like a kid, and more like an adult. By having allowed the fashion world to dictate to young children, we robbed them of their childhoods.

We saw in preceding chapters that even infants and young children are dressed up in the latest fashions and designer labels by their parents. The motive attributed to this behavior was that it is the parents who wish to make a statement about themselves. Parents with infants shop at stores like *Baby Gap* with an eye towards outfitting their young children in fashionable clothing. It is an act of self-definition for the parents – one whereby they hope to have their fashion awareness displayed to the world. What sense does it make to dress an infant in designer clothes, less it be to say something about the parents?

What about pre-teens? Do their parents shop for them? Is it normal for their clothing to be chosen for them by others? Do they have any say in what gets bought or what they wear? The answer is abundantly clear. Nowadays kids are very particular and they insist on choosing their own clothes. Even though it is the parents who open their wallets for merchandise bought for pre-teens, today it is the children themselves that do the shopping. This phenomenon represents another important development in the field of retail products for pre-teens and is one that cannot be overstated. This is where the real revolution has taken place because retailers are now selling *directly* to pre-teens, rather than to their parents. So, for advertisers and retailers, the problem becomes one of getting their message across to very young consumers.

When it comes to clothing, pre-teens have become relentless shoppers. They are probably far more persistent than adults, and are determined to buy exactly the products they want. Just look at any mall or children's clothing store and you will see very young shoppers, with parents in tow. The child shopper is a relatively new phenomenon but one that represents a very important and growing demographic. These shoppers represent a huge portion of the market and more importantly, they have ready access to their parent's cash when it comes to shopping.

Parents are very concerned about the welfare of their children. One of the principal things they worry about is that their children 'fit-in' among their peers. It is very important to parents that their children be popular and have friends. Unlike any time in the past, social acceptance now implies that in addition to being well liked, that the child has a sense of fashion awareness. Fitting-in is the bottom line. Although teens or adults may be more concerned with style or fashion, for pre-teens the emphasis is on blending in with friends and being one of the group. The concern is not to impress adults with fashion, but rather to conform to trends. The pre-teen shopper will be looking for anything that helps him fit in with his peers.

One key to this problem is to watch the teen market, for it is obvious that pre-teens, more than anything, emulate their older teen brethren when it comes to fashion. They regard teens as being exemplary of style, and the smart retailer will mimic teen fashions in his clothes for pre-teens. Similarly there is a tendency for kids to follow the example of teens when it comes to designer labels; the ones worn by the older group will soon be demanded by the younger group.

Boys shop with boys and girls shop with girls. The compartmentalization of stores into sections for the sexes is important. The girls do not want to be seen shopping by the boys, and the boys certainly do not want the girls to see them shopping. Separation is important.

Recent studies show that, for kids who are old enough to shop for themselves, there is a definite pattern to what they do. In particular what has been found is that, in the first instance, kids like to go browsing by themselves. They like to go out with their friends and reconnoiter the merchandise. What happens is that they then later bring their parents back to the same stores to actually buy the things they want. For the retailer this behavior makes a very important point. It may be tempting for the retailer to look at young kids shopping by themselves as little more than an annoyance or a waste of his time. They may appear to be too young to be ready to buy anything and so are regarded as just a nuisance. The point to make however is that even when pre-teens are browsing, they are probably doing so with an eye to bringing their parents back later to buy something. Thus the older child browser is important and should be viewed as a potentially serious shopper.

Are pre-teens controlled by their clothing? Any parent will be able to answer that question. The fashion industry has done an excellent job of creating fashion awareness among even the youngest of children, and the demand created in this group spurs even the youngest children to search endlessly for the correct clothing. Parents, wanting to be sure that their kids fit-in with their friends, go along with the obsession and are willing to go to great lengths and great expense to make sure their children get what they want.

What we are talking about here is shopping to define the personality. Even at the youngest ages, clothing has become much more than a practical necessity; it has become, instead, a status symbol and a rite of passage. Wearing the 'correct' clothing has become more important to pre-teens than just about anything else in their lives. There is no option. There is no alternative. They *must* wear clothing that is in style. They are social outcasts if they do not.

Pity the poor parent that tries to shop at discount chains to buy clothing at a bargain. We are at the point where pre-teens just will not tolerate such shopping anymore. Parents will be able to get away with this form of shopping for a few years, when kids are very young, but all too soon those children will become aware of fashion and style among their peers, and the discount shopping will end. Major chains that do not stock designer names and fashion labels are destined to lose market share, as the age at which children become brand aware continues to drop.

The pre-teen demographic is an important one. While parents age and become less concerned with fashion, a new marketing niche has opened among the youngsters. Strong demand has been created in a new demographic where it did not previously exist. The pre-teen shopper, with adult in hand, shops for the latest fashions and accessories. The parents, with wallets in hand, are willing to pay the price to ensure that their children are happy with their clothing. There has been a revolution in shopping and a big part of that revolution has been that the older child shopper has become a major influence in the retail market. If one needs to see proof of this phenomenon one just needs to look at the way in which any eight-year old is dressed. Most of them are regaled from head to toe in fashionable clothes that are covered in designer labels. Adults do not usually pay much attention to such dress, but to the young shopper his or her clothes are just about the most important thing in the world. This is an important demographic because the demand for products within the group is so intense. With young pre-teens, fashionable clothes and designer labels are no longer an option – they are an absolute necessity.

It is important to re-emphasise that young children are decision-makers. When one sees a parent and child shopping together, it is imperative to recognise that although it is the parent who is buying the product, it is the child who is making the decision. Retailers and advertisers need to direct their messages toward the child shopper, because he has far more decision-making power than is thought. It is hard to imagine that six or eight-year olds have become a dynamic shopping demographic, but that is exactly what has happened. This demographic has become one of the most important shopping units.

Entertainment: A Battleground for Kids and Parents

At the same time that there is a retailing revolution underway in the area of children's clothing, so too is there a revolution taking place in the field of children's entertainment. In the same way that adults are shopping at a higher level, so too are the kids when it comes to entertainment. Unfortunately, when it comes to choosing entertainment, kids and parents do not always agree. This is an awkward age for both parents and children alike. While parents still want to choose entertainment for a child that is wholesome and life-defining, young kids nowadays have different demands. The secret for the retailer of pre-teen entertainment is to come up with a product that satisfies both parent and child.

When it comes to entertainment for young children, Mom and Dad are still concerned with providing fare that is well rounded and healthy. Parents view their youngsters as little children and want them to have entertainment that is appropriate to their age. As far as they are concerned, entertainment, especially movies and television, should be family centered, rated G, and should be wholesome and amusing. Hopefully it is educational or moral as well. It should contain messages that are uplifting, honest, decent and honorable. *Barney* the dinosaur, a young child's television show, is typical of the type of entertainment that parents hope to provide for their young children. *Barney* is friendly, honest, caring, good spirited and an all around wonderful role model for children. Parents have very specific goals in mind when it comes to choosing entertainment for their children, and even if they do not verbalise these ideas, they are nevertheless very important when they make entertainment choices. For retailers it is important to be aware that parents have high hopes for their children and that they expect entertainment to be representative of those high hopes.

The kids have other ideas. They want entertainment that is exciting, thrilling and attention grabbing. At a very young age children want more sophisticated entertainment. They start to want to see grown-up fare, such as movies, that are popular with older groups. In the same way that young children emulate teens when they dress, so too they want to copy them when it comes to movies, television and other entertainment. It is not too long before young children are embarrassed to be seen at a *Disney* type movie with their parents. Even as young as six years of age, kids are starting to demand their own say in entertainment, and the freedom to choose what they want to see. *Barney* the dinosaur does not stay popular for very long.

Parents struggle with their children's desires. Battles ensue as very young children demand entertainment that parents feel is not appropriate for them. While the parents want them to watch a traditional *Disney* movie, the kids want to see the latest teen, gross-out comedy. Parents wrestle with the transformation that takes place. And the point for retailers is that the transformation is taking place at an ever-younger age. In the past, parents did not need to worry about such problems until their kids were in the teen years. But nowadays, the transformation takes place at a very young age and parents are faced with difficult decisions long before they hoped they had to make them.

Peer pressure plays a big role in pre-teen entertainment. Some parents may be against their children watching movies that are rated for a teen audience, with sexual content for example. Nevertheless if a trend develops, such that 'all the other kids' are going to watch the movie, what is the parent to do? As was the case with clothing, there is a balance here. On the one hand, the parents want what is best for their children and their development. They also do not want them to grow up too soon and hope to preserve the innocence of childhood as long as possible. On the other hand, there is the peer pressure of the child's friends. If the child is not permitted to see entertainment that all of his friends are allowed to see, he will perhaps be ostracized by the group and treated as a social outcast. Since this is the last thing in the world the parents want to see happen to their children, they almost always give in to the pressure and allow the child to do what he wants to do, even though they believe strongly that it is the wrong thing. The retailer should be aware that peer pressure plays an important role in the sales of entertainment. If part of the group can be sold a product that usually means that the whole group will end up consuming it. Advertisers can use peer pressure to sell entertainment products to pre-teens.

One might think that parents could get together and agree on a set of standards for a group of young friends. For example, the parents might agree that the group not be allowed to watch movies unless they are rated G. The problem with this approach is that there is always some parent who cannot say 'no'. This is the parent that is so anxious to please their child that they will let her watch whatever she pleases. Unfortunately, such parents set the standards for the whole group. If one of the children is allowed to watch a teen movie, this translates very quickly into the idea that 'all the other kids' are being allowed to do so. There are always some parents who cannot say 'no'.

Once the breach is broken, there is also no stopping the process. Once your child, and the group, has watched one teen movie, how can you reverse the process and not allow them to see the next one? Thus the process takes on its own life, with young kids being allowed to see one teen movie after another until there is no end to it. Suddenly, young children that the parents thought were innocent are watching every teen gross-out comedy that is on the market. The innocence of childhood is lost and young children end up watching entertainment that is well beyond their years. Their parents do not think it is right, but they also feel that their hands are tied. They sigh, they roll their eyes, and they throw up their hands in silent resignation.

Meanwhile, the movie and entertainment businesses do a booming business, having captured a whole new segment of the demographic market. The process that has been described above is just what the producers of entertainment want. Manufacturers of entertainment are always looking to increase their market share and, by extending their market into younger and younger demographic groups, they are able to do so. They constantly push the envelope of taste and decency farther and farther in the expectation of increasing market share. There is nothing sinister in their motives, they are simply doing what entrepreneurs do best, that is, selling more product. The standards that have been set in the entertainment industry are simply the end result of the capitalist process evolving to its natural conclusion in a particular business. Movie and television fare have not only become more adult for adults, they have also become more grown-up for kids. This is the industry's way of holding market share and of increasing sales of its products. Movie attendance is at an all time high.

From the perspective of shopping, the inevitable conclusion to be drawn is that consumers of entertainment are getting younger and younger. As time passes, parents will have less say in what their children demand for entertainment and the kids themselves become a more important market share. When that teen movie is marketed, the target audience is no longer the twelve to sixteen-year old group; rather it is the group that is between *six* and sixteen. Once again we see evidence that the child demographic is becoming an ever more important part of the shopping equation.

Just as was the case with clothing, the key to success with entertainment for pre-teens is to take the pulse of the teen group. As pre-teens become entertainment shoppers in their own right, it is especially with movies and television that they first start to make their own life-defining choices. In this process teen idols and teen movie stars become very important in determining what this group will want. The underlying concept is that this group just cannot wait to grow up and should therefore be targeted in almost the same way as the teen market. As shoppers they aspire to copy teenagers and so should be thought of as belonging to the same group. Ads that are targeted to sixteen-year olds should also be thought of as being directed to eight-year olds. There is less and less to distinguish between the two groups. Children should be thought of as young shoppers that are starting to make their own decisions about the entertainment that they buy.

Toys – A Shrinking Demographic

The retailing and manufacture of toys presents a challenge for the pre-teen market. Both sections above have suggested that the pre-teen demographic is becoming ever more sophisticated as a shopping group. The implication is that as children get more sophisticated the market for toys will shrink. There are two reasons for this. One is that as children grow up faster, they are less interested in toys. The other is that as children grow up sooner, the period of time during which they are interested in toys is diminishing.

One problem with toys is that there is little in-between ground. Either an item is a toy or it is not, and it is difficult to define something in between. The pre-teen demographic is a difficult one because it crosses two lines. Sometimes it is necessary to market to kids like they are just kids, and other times it is necessary to treat them as young adults.

Parents will be aware of the dilemma that is faced. For many years of childhood, parents spend a lot of time looking for toys for young children. Parents often enjoy this experience – it brings out the kid in everybody – and are normally delighted when they are about to buy toys that they think will please their children. The downside comes when the children start to get a little older. All of a sudden it seems the children have outgrown toys and the selection of items that parents can buy abruptly becomes very limited. Many parents will know the feeling of exasperation when their children have suddenly gotten too old for toys, and buying these as gifts, say at Christmas time, is no longer an option.

Children are growing up faster than they used to. The section on entertainment, for example, suggested how kids are being treated to more grown up fare when it comes to movies and television. This kind of lifestyle is making kids more grown up – more street-wise – at an earlier age than ever before. An important retail consequence of this is that kids are now less interested in the things that we traditionally associate with children, including toys. Nowadays even a six-year old will be a fan of a musical group like the *Backstreet Boys*. Given such a level of interest in things that are more 'grown up' it is difficult to imagine a continued interest in toys. Toy manufacturers need to look to new avenues of revenue, as young children grow more sophisticated.

From the retailer's perspective it is difficult if not impossible to create new toys that will appeal to older age groups. Toys are a very age specific product and therefore they have a limited demographic potential. Although a toy like *Barbie* is still a hot seller, and has a global market, the age at which girls will put away their *Barbies* is very young. Usually by seven or eight years of age the product has reached the end of its shelf life. Thus although the product is popular, it is limited to a very specific demographic group. Retailers are very unlikely to be able to extend the age of the appropriate demographic. In fact, the problem is exacerbated all the more when it is realized that the size of the demographic for toys is shrinking.

The length of childhood is becoming condensed. Toys imply 'play'. Twelve-year olds used to go outside just to play. Not any more. Play is not 'cool', it is only for little kids. Today's eight-year old is 'too cool' to go out to play. Rather they go to 'hang out' to be with friends. The implication is that childhood is shorter than it used to be. Kids used to stay in what could be called the childhood years for a longer time than they do now. Childhood used to last from approximately three to twelve-years of age, but now it lasts from about three to seven. Beyond that age kids feel they have to look grown-up, act grown-up and be grown-up.

For the toy market, the message is that the window of opportunity within which to sell toys to children is getting smaller. What used to be an eight or nine-year window of opportunity is now reduced to about five years. And it is getting shorter all the time. This is a declining market segment where it is difficult to create new demand. As childhood gets shorter, it gets more difficult to sell products to this demographic that is not only growing up faster, but is shrinking in size.

The enterprising manufacturer will redesign her products to make them appropriate to this grown-up demographic. A good example of this kind of approach was found in a recent product, *Boy Crazy!* It was a collection of trading cards featuring teenage boys that sold to young girls. It was described as one of the hottest fads to hit the market. Girls could buy sets of nine cards for $3.50 that made up part of a set of cards. The cards featured average, non-threatening, everyday boys that the girls found attractive. *Boy Crazy!* represented an excellent example of the toy market adjusting to the new realities of the pre-teen demographic. More sophisticated products like this are just what is needed to spur demand in this segment.

What do toys provide for the young child? In the previous discussion of toys for toddlers, it was indicated that for very young children parents want toys that stimulate thought, development and creativity. They want toys that shape and mold the personality and those that turn an infant into a better young person. What do parents of six to twelve-year olds want when it comes to 'toys' or other non-clothes items for their children? An important consideration at this age becomes the goal of fitting in with friends. Thus if the friends own *Barbies* or *GI Joes*, it is important to parents that their children do so as well. Even at a very young age peer pressure starts to play a big role in the shopping decisions that parents will make. For retailers it is important to be able to gauge trends and fads in the marketplace and to stay in step with the latest popular products. There is almost a herd mentality when it comes to buying the hottest items for children, and almost everyone will be aware of the fads that sweep through this demographic. There is an endless list of products over the years like *Cabbage Patch Dolls*, *Beanie Babies* and so on that become hot-selling novelties in the market for a time. It is important for the retailer to 'catch the wave' when such products hit the shelves.

In spite of the coercion of peer pressure, there is also a strong desire on the part of parents to please their children when they buy them things. This means that very often practicality and educational value go out the window as parents try simply to buy things that will please their children. Every parent will be familiar with the feeling of buying toys that have no redeeming value but that are just for fun, excitement or adventure. Parents often struggle with these conflicting goals for toys but can find a happy medium by buying a mixture of items, some of which have redeeming value and some of which are just for entertainment. From the retailer's point of view it is important to have toy products that are high quality, attention grabbing and sellable just because they look like fun.

Sexist Shopping and Products

Toys are sexist. Despite the laments of those who decry the sexual stereotypes that still exist with toys, the market itself remains firmly and indeed vigorously sexist. Girls still get dolls and boys get trucks. Some parents will try to break down the barriers by buying toys of the 'wrong' gender for their children. Thus we have dolls designed for boys and trucks designed for girls. But such purchases represent the exception rather than the rule. Most shoppers are still firmly committed to shopping in the stereotypical sexist tradition. In fact if we go by shopping patterns it seems clear that most people believe strongly that buying toys of the 'correct' gender is an important part of molding personality and shaping the child. Sales of merchandise that is decidedly and purposely sexist are higher than ever. Clearly parents prefer toys that clearly identify their children's gender.

Why is there such a sexist difference between children? Studies show in fact that given a choice, boys prefer masculine type toys and girls prefer feminine type toys. Why does this difference persist? One theory holds that the difference is attributable to different levels of testosterone in the sexes. Thus even young boys have testosterone and have far more of it than girls. This is said to lead to the 'unique' behaviors that are attributable to the sexes such as greater aggression among boys and more caring type behavior among girls. This is an interesting theory for the retail component of this demographic because it says there are real reasons for the differences between the sexes and that retailers, manufacturers and advertisers should do their utmost to exploit those differences. There are natural, biological reasons for the differences and this means that products that strike a particular chord with children of one sex or another are likely to be more successful than others.

Interestingly, some manufacturers are using the difference between the sexes to sell items even when there is no real difference between the male and female versions of the products. One recent marketing campaign sold '*Barbie* computers' for girls and '*Hot Wheels* computers' for boys, even though the products themselves were virtually identical. They even made the two computers in pink and blue. This is often a stroke of marketing genius and it can double the sales of a single existing product. In other words, if a family has a boy and a girl, the retailer can sell two versions of the same product to the family – one for each sex. The girl will not want to use the boy's blue computer, nor will the boy want to use the girl's pink computer. This is a simple way to boost sales, yet most parents, anxious to please their kids, do not see through it. The number of orders for *Hot Wheels* and *Barbie* computers was such that the manufacturer could not keep up with demand.

Exploiting the difference between the sexes – even when the difference is artificial – is an old idea. Accolades should go to the manufacturer that first suggested that the simple bicycle should be available in a 'boys' version and a 'girls' version. This bit of sales acumen immediately doubled the sale of bicycles. Girls did not want to ride boy's bikes, and boys would not be caught dead on a girl's bike, even though the difference between the two was trivial. Certainly there are many other areas where it is possible to identify different versions of the same product for the sexes and to exploit this as an effective marketing tool.

Consider as one simple example of this idea, the prospect of selling children's swing sets in boy and girl versions. To date this product has been sold largely in a generic version, where it is of interest to both sexes. But one can easily imagine a girls swing set in pink, with appropriate accessories, and a boys swing set in blue, with attachments designed for boys. Presumably the boys and girls would be loath to use the swing set of the opposite sex. Although this sounds like a sales strategy that is self-serving in the extreme, and a setback to women's rights, this approach is absolutely no different than what is accepted, everyday practice with bicycles. And, from the retailer's point of view, it is a strategy that will double the sales of a product.

As another everyday example of the marketing of different versions of the same product to the sexes, think of the case of clothing. Here is an area where even pink and blue baby sleepers cannot be used inter-changeably among the sexes. The difference between men and women's clothing persists at all age levels and ensures that sales are strong among both sexes. What other products are there that could be *sexualized*? This is a simple way to increase retail sales that has a great deal of potential that may be currently going unexploited.

Sports and Activities

The years from five or six to about twelve or thirteen are the years for kids' outdoor activities. This is the time in life when parents try to define their children through the everyday behavior they carry out. Soccer, piano lessons, baseball, art classes, swimming, basketball, skiing and so on are all activities in which parents enroll their kids, presumably 'for their own good'. In most cases these activities represent the desires of the parents more than the children, but nevertheless children are anxious to participate because at this age they are still very anxious to please their parents. The self-centered teen mentality has not yet taken hold.

Many such activities involve purchases. In one sense the activities themselves often have to be paid for. Usually parents are keen to participate regardless of cost and often the costs of participation are offset by various fundraising activities organized by parents and groups. From another perspective there is the retail side of organized activities. Almost every sport requires equipment of some sort and this is a retail area of significance. In most cases parents are anxious for their children to do well in their activities and often this means that price is no object when it comes to outfitting children for sports.

There is a large amount of pressure placed on pre-teens when it comes to organized activities. Parents unknowingly take the perspective that their child's performance and abilities reflect on themselves. There is an enormous competition factor at work. A parent is thrilled when his son or daughter hits a home run. Not only does the child feel a sense of success and accomplishment, but also so do the parents. They are proud of their child and they are especially pleased that he or she has performed well in a competitive environment. Parents live and die with their child's performance in an activity, and sub-par performance usually means that words of encouragement are necessary, as are extra practice sessions.

One seemingly good way to encourage the maximum performance from your child is to buy him or her the very best equipment possible. Smart retailers are already aware of this factor and do their utmost to exploit the emotional concerns of anxious parents. An expensive ball glove is a good investment if it makes the child perform well in front of his peers and other adults. If he catches that important fly ball, the price of the glove becomes insignificant compared to the emotional well-being that is engendered by success. That expensive batting glove is worth every dollar if the child hits a big home run while wearing it. The retail market for equipment for sports and organized activities for kids is an important one because it depends largely on the emotional investment of parents.

The world of designer labels and brand names has also entered the sporting world in a way that is unprecedented. Even young children are well aware of brand names when it comes to sports equipment and, when it comes to participating, only those brand names will do. The best known of these names is *Nike*, which has established a presence in many sports, but every sport today has associated with it several well-known brand names which are 'must have' for both parents and children alike. There are big stakes at risk in kid's activities and only the best equipment will do. Parents are more than willing to pay the higher price for brand names because they believe it will help their child to succeed. And that, after all, is the bottom line.

Retailers and advertisers can exploit the emotional anxiety of parents and children alike. There is nothing quite like the stress for a child of trying to perform in a competitive environment, in front of an audience, while trying to please one's parents. Talk about pressure. Advertising campaigns should emphasize the important role of the equipment in ensuring success for child and parent in the activity. When it comes to organized activities, parents and kids are shopping at a higher level than they used to. Today the proper equipment is seen to be crucial to achievement and more often than not a proper brand name is part of the equation. Shoppers are willing to pay whatever price it takes to ensure success.

Mini-Teens

The fashion industry reaches into the hearts and minds of pre-teens. There is little to stop the onslaught, as parents, anxious to please their children, are active and willing participants in the process. The end result is the creation of a demographic class that might best be called the *mini-teens*. These are pre-teens that have become miniature teenagers in their dress and in their activities. These are kids that just cannot wait to grow up. Even the idea of *girl power*, popularized by the *Spice Girls*, translates down into the very youngest age groups.

Retailers and advertisers need to sense that the pre-teen demographic is childlike no more. Today's six-year olds are into the same interests in music, clothes, activities and entertainment as are sixteen-year old teens. If you really want to get a sense of how things have changed, just talk to a school gym teacher. What they will tell you is that it is almost impossible to get kids to participate in sports and activities. Boys, and especially girls, now feel they are just 'too cool' to get involved in a school game or sport. Such activities are regarded as being suitable for 'little kids' who do not know any better.

Another good example of the changing tide of sentiment in the pre-teen years comes from the media. It reports that the participation of boys in the sport of competitive swimming has been on the decline, in spite of more and better facilities being available for this activity. The reason given for this declining participation? The answer is that the boys do not want to wear or be seen in the *Speedo* type of trunks that competitors wear. They are not 'cool'.

The swimming example is a good illustration of the kinds of frustration that will be faced by marketers and advertisers when it comes to the pre-teen demographic. Kids are very fussy about what they wear, and what they do, and there is literally nothing that can be done to change such attitudes. The fashion and entertainment industries have done an excellent job of creating mini-teens.

Chapter 5

Teens:
Shopping for an Identity

Is there a more difficult, interesting, intriguing demographic than the teen one? Teens have come to dominate society in many ways. They have their own movies. Teen gross-out comedies are one of the largest draws at the box office. They have their own music. Teen groups and songs dominate radio play and the airwaves. They have their own clothing. Walk into a typical clothing store in a mall and it seems like everything they have on display is designed for sixteen-year olds. Why is this demographic so important, why does it command the attention it does, and how can retailers better understand how it works?

The answer is in sales. Even though the teen demographic does not seem that large in size, it is big in its marketing clout. The total disposable income of this group is in the billions of dollars. Teens get attention because they are important consumers. They do not have a lot of things to buy but they are very selective in what they purchase. While adults buy a variety of different items – from lawnmowers to furniture – teens are much more restricted in the items for which they shop. Their interests are limited to just a few areas – primarily clothing, entertainment, and food – yet in those few areas their numbers belie their importance. There are some sectors of the economy where teens just dominate, and their considerable influence cannot be ignored.

The Teen Shopping Mentality

Are teens aware of their marketing significance? They probably do not give it a second thought. They are mostly aware of style and fashion and they believe that anyone over twenty years of age is hopelessly out-of-date. Young teens have discovered style and fashion for the first time in their lives, and so everything is new to them. They believe strongly that they are the only ones who really dress in fashion.

Teens have attitude. For the first time in their lives it becomes apparent to them that they can have thoughts, ideas, and even clothes that are new, unique, and the product of their own desires. This new self-centeredness gives them an attitude of confidence. Teen attitude is also engendered by the fact that they are young and healthy, and so firmly believe that they are invincible. They do not have the responsibilities of adulthood. Can you explain all of this to them? Of course not. Teens feel very strongly that they are independent and they feel they should be treated like young adults. They think their voice should be heard. They demand their freedom, they demand ever more products and they demand that their parents pay for it. Their shopping and buying habits reflect their self-indulgent attitude. There is a mentality to the teen years that is like no other and it is important for retailers to understand it.

How does a retailer market to a demographic that has such a mindset? The answer is to be found partly in the idea that teens are now shopping and buying products without their parents and so are experiencing all of the emotions and uncertainties of shopping for the very first time. Shopping on their own is new to them and so they are persistent and dedicated shoppers. The retailer has to try to imagine what it is like being a novice shopper, where everything is a first-time experience. The retailer can, to some extent, approach the teen shopper as inexperienced and naïve but only for a limited time. For the teen shopper, the shopping process is a learning process. They are fast learners. They quickly discover the relationship between price and quality, and between value and product worth. After just a few expeditions they become seasoned shoppers.

Teens shop with an attitude that is unique. In particular what sets them apart from the adult shopping demographic is that they usually have a surplus of time. Teen shoppers have patience because, unlike harried adults who are time-pressed, they have lots of leisure time for shopping. This is especially true for young teens that do not work part-time. They have all of the hours of after-school time, evenings and weekends to devote to shopping. They have *surplus time* – in fact, they have so much of it that they undoubtedly shop sometimes just to pass the time. It is difficult for most adults to remember a time when they had so much leisure time for shopping. For teens, shopping becomes a part of *recreation* – *s*omething they do to unwind, relax and pass the hours.

For retailers the message is clear. Teen shoppers will be among the fussiest, difficult to please customers with which they deal. Teens will be extremely aware of competitor's prices and products because they have the time to carry out serious comparison-shopping. They have the time and the patience to be wary and well-informed shoppers. The enterprising retailer has to be on her toes if she is to market successfully to the teen demographic. It is not to be taken lightly.

Just like the pre-teens discussed in the preceding chapter, teens also have a tendency to reconnoiter the goods they want. In other words, when it comes to buying a product, a teen shopper often has the time to carry out a reconnaissance mission. The item that is wanted will be perused at several locations and price and quality will be noted. Only later will the teen shopper come back to actually purchase the item. Retailers who see teens browsing probably often assume incorrectly that they browse simply because they cannot afford to buy. Nothing could be farther from the truth. Teen browsing is simply the first stage in the process of teen shopping. In fact, teens may look at a particular product several times before they commit to buying it.

The Time World of Teens

Teens live in a different world than adults. One of the biggest differences between adults and teens is in their perception of time. In particular, adults live in a world where time goes by faster, while teens live in one where time unfolds at a slower pace. Consider an example. For the parents of teenagers the four years of high school seem to go by quickly. Those four years seem like an instant from the perspective of the adults. But from the teen point of view, the four years of high school seem like an eternity. They live in a time world where it seems like a long time for next weekend to come, let alone for four years to go by. Adult readers of this book will remember their own four years of high school as seeming to last forever.

How does the teen's perception of time affect their shopping behavior? The bottom line is that they are likely to shop more often than adults. For example, when an adult buys a shirt they may expect it to last for a couple of years, but for a teen such a time scale is totally unrealistic. A teen is more likely to see a shirt as an item that has a life of maybe a year or a half-year. There is quite a different perspective on time from the two points of view. Similarly, an adult might buy a pair of shoes with the expectation that they will be worn to work for a year but before they know it, three years has gone by and they are still wearing the same old shoes. For a teen, the world cycles according to the school year and so everything new seems old at the start of a new academic year, if not every semester.

What are the implications for the retailer of the different time world of the teen? The answer is that product turnover has to be faster for teens than it is for adults. Merchandise displays need to be rotated and updated far more quickly for teens than for adults. At the same time, store advertisements will have to be updated faster for the teen demographic. A retailer might put up a new display in a store and expect that once the job is done it will last for months. But for the teen shopper, frequent trips to the store means that the display becomes dated very quickly. The adult retailer has to be aware of the different time perception of her teen clientele.

Leading edge retailers will also be cognizant of the time world of teens when it comes to product change. While adults will have a long-range view of the world, teens from their perspective, will see things differently. Merchandise has to turn over frequently for the recurrent teen shopper. The teens that shop today will be back again in a week looking for new and interesting merchandise. For the adult it may be months between visits to the store.

Products expire faster for the teen demographic. For an adult, a purchased music CD may have a shelf life of several months, if not a year, while for a teen a CD reaches its expiry date in weeks. The same kind of logic applies to all teen purchases and so the wise retailer will be prepared to try to think in terms of *teen time* and will update products and displays accordingly.

The *Teen Timescape* and Brand Names

Are teens loyal to brands? In some cases it seems that they are. A good example is found in the case of the *Nike* brand that was a teen favorite for many years. For a long period of time you could not see a teen that was not wearing the distinctive *Nike* 'Swoosh' somewhere on his clothing. But every brand has a limited shelf life and even the *Nike* brand has started to lose its appeal. Studies show that the brand is slowly falling out of favor with the teen demographic. This shows that in the time world of teens, even brand loyalty only lasts for so long.

When it comes to brand names it is important again to appreciate the unique time world of teens. Consider basketball great Michael Jordan, who retired just a few years ago. While adults and older teens can still relate to Jordan and his athletic accomplishments, there is now a whole new generation of young teens that never heard of him and do not remember him. Today's twelve-year old will have been only eight-years old when Jordan was at his peak. What seems like just yesterday to an adult will seem like ancient history to the teen demographic. To a twelve-year old the world is a fresh new place and everything in it is new and never before experienced. The brand names and fashion labels that are seen by young teens are, for them, the only ones that ever existed. The *mental timescape* of teens is unfamiliar and unseen by adults who have longer memories than teens. A new brand name is a novelty to a teen and something that they see as 'belonging' to them. It is even better if the new name is unknown by adults – that makes it all the more special to the teen.

Retailers, manufacturers and advertisers need to appreciate the unique time world of the teen demographic. This is a group that has no history. Everything is new and novelty is a big part of the attraction to these first-time shoppers. They do not want to wear the brand names that their older brothers and sisters wear, let alone the ones that their parents wear. *Levi* jeans represent a good example of the dating of a brand name. To the teen demographic, *Levi* jeans are "the jeans your parents wear". Today's teenager will want his or her own brand of jeans to wear. Having their own unique brand is more important to them than the product itself. It is part of the process of self-definition for the teen. Shopping for the first time means establishing an identity and defining the personality through the items purchased. Retailers would be wise to keep producing new brand names every couple of years in the hope of putting on a fresh face for a teen demographic that wants to reinvent itself every year.

The examples above show that there is a shorter product cycle for the teen demographic. Fashion labels and brand names that become popular can only hold their place as long as a generation of teens is loyal to them. After just four years the entire high school student body changes and so do the fashions and trends that go with it. Just think of the huge time gaps in high school. The time span from being a freshman to being a senior seems so large as to be almost endless when you are a teen, and the four years of high school seems like a whole lifetime when you are just sixteen-years old. Retailers need to remember that a generation in the teen years is just a few years long, and in that period of time, what was once the hottest style in town can quickly become dated and obsolete. The teen demographic lives in a world that has its own properties of time. Many retailers and advertisers should take into account the unique teen perspective when they design and promote their products. The speed, scale and shifting of time in the teen world are unlike that of any other demographic.

The Obsession with Designer Labels

Are teens obsessed about brand names and designer labels? They certainly appear to be. The fashion industry has again done an exceptional job in its ability to grab the minds and hearts of teens. Teens seem to be overpowered and controlled by their focus on brand names and this seems to be a trend that is only getting stronger through time. Why are teens so obsessed with designer labels and fashions? What is it about this phenomenon that so captures the souls of teens?

Part of the answer is found in the teen obsession with belongingness and group identity. In the introduction, Maslow's Hierarchy of Human Needs was introduced and a corresponding arrangement of Levels of Shopping was portrayed (Figure 1.1). Belongingness is one of a set of human needs that is essential to psychological well-being. The fact that teens 'dress to belong' is not just an obsession but rather is part of a complex web of behaviors. It enables teens to maintain a healthy feeling about their place in the world and their relationship to friends and, indeed, to all other teens. When a teen walks into a social event, such as a concert, and sees hundreds of others dressed in the same way as she is, it does not cause her embarrassment or awkwardness – rather it causes feelings of self-worth, group identity and a profound sense of personal identification and belongingness that is central to feeling good about oneself.

What the fashion industry has done is quite an accomplishment. They have been able to exploit a fundamental human need for belongingness by using brand names as a vehicle to group identity. It is not the fashion label that is important – it is the group membership that it creates that really matters. It is like buying a membership in a social club where one wears special clothing – a shirt or a jacket – that proclaims one's membership in the club. For teens this is accomplished just by buying the right clothes with the right labels. Teens have long been concerned with dressing according to group norms. In fact this is a behavior that can be traced back a long time. The relatively recent appearance of designer labels on teen clothing just adds another way in which teens can ensure their membership in a group. Previously this had to be done just with clothing, for example, saddle shoes or Poodle skirts in the 1950s, but in the modern era the fashion industry has exploited the need for belongingness by adding a whole new level to the concept. By focusing on designer labels, on everything from shoes to sunglasses, the industry has created a new way to demonstrate group membership. Teens are very brand aware and this is simply because the brand names provide a vehicle that creates an instant sense of group identity.

How long are teens loyal to a fashion label? The answer is that it depends on the consensus of the group as a whole. There is an unwritten understanding among teens about what is 'in' and what is not. Word spreads quickly when fashions change and when styles are lost. How do they know? To the adult, it seems as if teens have invisible fashion radar that keeps them informed of the latest trends. The truth of the matter is that it is television, social events, concerts, magazines and especially word of mouth that keep teens informed of the latest fads. How it all works is through what we can call a bandwagon effect. Teens see other teens with a new style or item of dress and before long they adopt the new innovation themselves. A good example is found in the trend toward waistless jeans that girls have adopted. These are jeans without a waistband. The trend is said to have started when pop star Mariah Carey went backstage and cut the waistband off of her jeans just before a concert. That started the trend – teens copied other teens – and before long manufacturers were providing store-bought jeans with no waistband. The whole process only took a couple of months. The ability of teens to propagate a new idea – and the ability of the fashion industry to respond – is nothing short of incredible. Teens have a vast and complex web of communications that is overwhelmingly effective when it comes to conveying information about trends and fashions.

Fashion trends come and go swiftly in the time world of teens and usually adults find it impossible to keep up with the latest teen styles. This is the way teens want it to be. The fashions should be unique and individual to them – they should be their own and not something that is borrowed or dated. Teen styles should evaporate quickly – they should disappear as fast as they are invented, with an ever-changing façade that keeps styles as fresh and innovative as possible. It is the challenge to the retailer and the advertiser to keep pace with the timescape of the teen world.

The obsession with brand names goes well beyond clothing. Whether it is snowboards, bicycles, or car audio systems, the important thing to teens is the brand name. Not only does buying a brand name create a sense of belonging, it also creates a sense of personal satisfaction and pleasure in the buyer. Teen shoppers have been conditioned by industry and by peers to accept the idea that the *only* suitable products are ones with an appropriate brand name. Shopping mentality has changed. Although brand names are certainly not new – they have been around as long as products have – there is a new mindset in the teen shopper that not only says that virtually every product has to have an appropriate brand name, but also that peer pressure dictates that the only acceptable products are those with brand names. Retailers such as *Wal-Mart*, which try to compete for the most part with no-name clothing products, are missing out on a large share of the brand name market.

While there are some brand names that have long lives – such as *Nike* or *Adidas* – there are others that are short-lived in their time spans. The number of different jean manufacturers whose brand names come and go among teens pays testament to the fact that some designer labels have a very short shelf life. A company that has achieved brand name status has to work very hard to keep that brand name front and center or else be doomed to market marginalization as the next fad sweeps the nation. Teens are not fickle, as the standard line goes. Rather they are conditioned by advertising and promotion. A brand can retain its importance so long as it has a successful marketing strategy.

The successful retailer who is targeting teens will carry the latest fashion labels and brand names. The successful advertiser will focus on brand association as the fundamental element of any marketing campaign. The central and significant role of branding and designer labeling in the modern economy cannot be understated. We are living and shopping in an age when the label on the product is far more important than the product itself. Any retailer who believes otherwise is fooling himself. It is the *age of the brand name.*

Over the past couple of decades branding has been extended into new areas. A few years ago there were areas that were untouched by brand names, for example eyeglasses, but now the forces of product identification have visited virtually every product. A good example of this trend is found in underwear. In years past, people were indifferent about the brand of underwear they bought. Today, designer label underwear has become big business as teens have become brand aware even in this area of clothing. Underwear used to be something that your Mom bought, but today it is unacceptable for teens to wear anything but designer brand undergarments. This trend is all the more interesting when it is noted that prices for such fashionable underwear are usually far higher than those for generic brands. This makes a clear statement that young consumers are willing to pay higher prices for designer label products of any nature. The question that retailers and manufacturers need to ask is whether there are other product lines where new demand can be created by branding products that previously have not been branded. This is a difficult challenge, of course, because virtually every area imaginable has been successfully branded, but there always remains the possibility that there exists new territories that are as yet uncharted by designer labels. A good example might be toothpaste, for instance, which still sells in the usual old brand names with which we are all familiar. Can teens be sold on toothpaste with a designer label? Undoubtedly the answer is 'yes' they can.

Clothing – A Teen Thing?

Are teens obsessed with clothing? From all appearances they certainly seem to be. Why is this so? Most adults would suggest that this is just a 'phase' that teens go through and that, as they grow older, the obsession will pass.

Nothing could be farther from the truth. The fact of the matter is that adults are just as obsessed about their clothing, as are teens. Just look at how the men dress in any office – shirts, ties, jackets – they all look like they belong to a club. How can anyone accuse teens of wearing a uniform when they are compared to a group of middle management office workers?

There are a few good reasons why teens should be obsessed with clothes. The most important one is that for the first time in their lives they are able, as shoppers, to start to define themselves through their clothing. All through their lives they have had clothes picked out for them by their parents or they have been forced to go shopping with their parents. Now for the first time, they are shopping on their own and *making decisions on their own*. This is a huge step for teens because they are starting to make choices about their own lives. How they look and how they dress is entirely up to their own making. This presents a freedom of choice to teens that they never before have experienced. To them, it is unique and retailers should be aware of this fact.

Clothing is all about defining the self and for teens the opportunity to shop represents a first-time opportunity to start to define themselves. They are making decisions without their parents and this represents a big first step towards adulthood and freedom. Adults do not appreciate the significance of shopping to teens. To ascribe their concern with clothes to a 'phase' is an insulting way to describe this important stage of life. As teens set out to break free of the control of parents, and start to establish themselves as unique, the first opportunity to do so comes with choosing their own clothing. Teen clothing represents much more than style, fashion and fad. In all truth it represents the first opportunity for teens to self-define.

A second reason why teens focus on clothing is a practical one. On their limited budgets this is all they can afford to define themselves. Adults can buy houses, cars, furnishings and other big-ticket items when they want to make a statement about themselves. Teens need to define themselves on a limited budget and at the age they are at, clothing fits the bill.

A third reason why teens should be obsessed with clothes has already been discussed. The reason is found in their need to belong. Teens are no different than adults when it comes to this need and, in fact, it is possible to suggest that for the young, inexperienced teen there is a *greater* need to belong than for adults. By buying the 'right' clothes, teens buy membership in social groups and establish relationships with friends. Shopping to belong is about shopping to establish peer group and personal identity and is one of the most important of human behaviors. This is shopping at the third level.

There is more to teen shopping than just shopping to belong however. Looking at the levels of shopping identified in the introduction, teens also shop for reasons of self-esteem. At the fourth level of shopping, teens will shop to create feelings of self-image or self-respect. This will include shopping for items, such as clothing or accessories that instill feelings of self-worth and confidence. How is this possible? The answer is found in the fact that buying products, especially those that are in style, creates inner feelings of self-esteem. Everyone knows the feelings when a special item of clothing is purchased, that is, a sense of feeling good about oneself. Shopping is an important vehicle to feelings of self-esteem and retailers, and especially advertisers, should be aware of these deeper levels of the shopping experience. Having the latest fashion in shoes or clothes is about more than being in style. It is also about being able to feel good about yourself and the fashions you own. Confidence and feelings of personal satisfaction result from teen shopping and the wise retailer is prepared to cater to needs at these levels.

At the fifth level, teens will shop for reasons of self-actualization. This involves shopping at the highest level, where the goal is to achieve feelings of self-fulfillment or deep personal satisfaction. This is shopping that goes beyond the need for belonging and beyond the need for self-esteem. Shopping for reasons of self-actualization is shopping to satisfy the soul. Such feelings come about, for example, when a product is purchased that is for the self and for self-indulgence. An example might be the teen shopper who buys a CD or a poster for their room. It is not the price of the item that counts in self-actualizing shopping, but the reason for buying it. It is not to impress friends and it is not to create feelings of self-esteem. Rather it is something that the shopper buys 'just for herself' to satisfy inner emotions. A special book of poetry or a new necklace might fulfill the same role – it is a purchase that is strictly for the inner self.

How does the retailer or advertiser tap into shopping at the fifth level? It is not easy. There is a subtle sense to this kind of shopping and it is one that is fleeting. Perhaps the best that can be said is that the retailer should look beyond the everyday basic needs of his customers and try to stock products that satisfy emotional needs. This is a difficult challenge but certainly represents an approach that is unique and intriguing to the buyer. As for advertising, it becomes clear that those creating ads should direct themselves to the higher order, and unstated, needs of their customers. An ad campaign that shows the features of a new automobile, for example, does not address itself to the deeper inner needs of teen shoppers. Advertisers have to shoot for a higher level of emotion than they often do at present. There is a whole different world of psychological needs of shoppers that is not being met.

It is clear that sometimes all of the levels of shopping appear to be rolled into one. A pair of jeans satisfies basic survival needs, provides a sense of belonging, increases self-esteem and may also function as a source of self-fulfillment. As has been said previously, the difference between the levels of shopping is in the mind of the shopper. The retailer should look at the nondescript shopper as a possible candidate for shopping at any one of the levels; any given shopper may be functioning at any level. What is important is to realize that the levels exist and to relate them to the individual shopper. From the teen perspective this distinction is all the more important given that most shopping focuses on clothing and accessories.

Why do teens seem to wear exactly the same clothes that their friends wear? As they define themselves, they have two goals. One is to belong, to be part of a group, while the other is to be an individual, distinct from others. Wearing the so-called uniform of their peer group, while simultaneously expressing individualism, accomplishes both goals. They all seem to wear the same thing but, much like adults, they each declare their uniqueness by the subtle variations (color, cut, style) in what they wear. Teens like to be unique. Although it may not appear that way to adults, teens will define themselves as individuals by the clothes they wear. A special necklace, a unique pair of earrings, a different watch, a distinct hairstyle, can all serve to make a statement about individuality, in spite of trends to conformity.

The Clothes Shopping Gap

The teen demographic is important. Most stores seem to carry clothes that are overwhelmingly directed to teens. Adults shopping in many mall stores and even large department stores are made to feel old, and out of place, as 'young' fashions and styles dominate the displays. In reality there seems to be just two kind of clothes on the market, namely those for teens and then those for everybody else. Older shoppers are hard-pressed to find fashions and styles that seem youthful but that do not make them look silly. Many adults try to emulate teen styles only to find that no matter how hard they try, they cannot keep up. Look around the malls and you will see middle-aged women trying to wear the latest teen style. They look awkward. Worse yet is the middle-aged male who tries to wear those baggy jeans. The styles are obviously for teens and the middle-aged shopper who tries to fit in just looks out of place. Most clothing stores cater to the youth market and whether they are aware of it or not, they leave older shoppers cold. At the same time, shopping for clothes is easy for teens. Everything is made for them, fits them, and looks good on them. They are unaware of their own importance in the marketplace and it is only later in life that this reality sets in. Typically this occurs when a teen reaches young adulthood and begins a job. Suddenly the teen fashions that have been worn for years will no longer be acceptable and the young shopper is forced to confront the realities of the adult fashion world. Simply there is nothing to choose between but youthful teen fashions and 'old people' clothes. It is at this stage of life that the harsh realities of growing up confront the young shopper head on. One wonders how many retailers are aware of the important transition that takes place and how many attempt to supply clothing to the in-between market that exists? All teens have to face the day when they suddenly are confronted with buying grownup clothing. Are the stores ready to give them what they want?

The huge chasm that exists between the teen shopper and the middle-aged shopper is called *the clothes shopping gap*. There seems to be little being accomplished to fill this gap even though it presents a huge potential market to manufacturers and retailers.

Entertainment

Teen entertainment is big. Teens have their own television shows, their own magazines, their own movies, their own radio stations and their own web sites. As is the case with clothing, sometimes teens seem to dominate the marketplace. Just look at prime time television for instance. The airwaves are dominated by shows that are directed entirely to teenagers. New marketing arrangements that link those television shows to brand names are in fashion. For example, on the hit teen show *Dawson's Creek* the designer label worn by the teen stars is *American Eagle Outfitters*. Similarly with movies, there exists a whole teen genre that leads the marketplace. Teen movies are so popular they are regularly in the top ten of movies that are being shown. Hollywood makes movies just for teenagers. New releases hit the theatres and there are certain pictures that are 'must see' for teens.

For teens the essential part of movies is that it is a shared entertainment experience. This is shopping to belong. Teens invariably go to a movie with a group of friends and so the sharing of the movie is essential for its success. Hollywood producers need to focus on this element if they wish to be successful – the movie has to generate debate and dialogue for it to be a hit among teens. It has to engender participation. They have to come out of the theatre sharing it with their friends and wanting to talk more about it. A movie that does not spur conversation is seen to be dull. This probably explains the great lengths to which Hollywood producers are going to create so-called teen gross-out comedies. These certainly give their audiences something to talk about. The people who are making teen movies are constantly pressing the envelope of taste and censorship. There is a good reason for this. In order to catch teens' attention and get them talking about a movie, it has to extend the boundaries and go beyond its predecessors. It has to reach new heights of extreme entertainment to capture the interest of its teen audience. It is only in this way that sharing and belongingness become a reality.

The same element of sharing, and shopping to belong, exists for teen television as well as for movies. The most important component of watching a hit teen television show is in the ability to share the experience with friends. Even if the show is actually watched in isolation, the important thing is to be able to talk about it later with schoolmates. Thus successful shows will cause conversation to emerge and after-show dialogue to develop. To do this they must be interesting, challenging, controversial or deeply emotional. A perfect example of this phenomenon was the hit series *Survivor* that, at its zenith, was a hot topic of conversation. Thus teens shop for television shows because they create a sense of belongingness.

Advertisers need to pay strict attention to the theme that teens shop first and foremost to satisfy needs for belongingness. Ads that are directed to this emotional component of the teen mentality are likely to succeed where others fail. Teens shop mostly at the third level and advertisements which exploit this phenomenon will be the most effective. This is the whole secret of brand names and designer labels and the same principles can be employed effectively when it comes to advertising other products.

Magazines represent another area where teens have their say. In the last few years a number of new teen magazines have been placed on the market that trade on the well-established name of a parent magazine to make their mark. *Teen People* and *Cosmo Girl* are two examples of this trend. At what level of shopping is buying a magazine? In the case of teens, magazines also fulfill the role of shopping to belong. In most cases there are 'how to' articles on topics such as attracting the opposite sex and in addition there is an emphasis on celebrities and stars. Reading these magazines is a way for kids to keep up with trends and styles but is also mostly about fitting in with friends who also read them. Sharing the same magazines creates a sense of belongingness and group identity. Producers of these products need to keep in mind the shared experience when they develop their product. More generally, reading a magazine that is directed to a segment of the market is about creating an identity with that market. The girl who reads *Seventeen* magazine is not just reading a magazine. She is identifying with a whole demographic group that reads the same magazine and this is very important to the psychology of the process. This is not just shopping to belong to a local group; rather it is shopping to belong to a demographic.

Radio stations present an interesting dilemma. Although teens have traditionally been big users of the radio this pattern is changing as the importance of the Internet grows. More and more teens are using the Internet to tune into radio stations from all over the world. The Internet expands the scope of their listening from local broadcasters to Internet stations from literally anywhere on earth. As the popularity of this medium grows, local broadcasters are going to have a more challenging job to get young listeners to tune in. According to a study by Edison Media Research, Internet radio sites are attracting the twelve to twenty-four year old demographic group in record numbers.

Why is the radio, including Internet radio, so popular with teens? Once again it is clear that the answer is found in the need to belong. Teens share songs and share the common experience of music. It is 'cool' to know all the words and to be able to sing along, not only with the radio, but with your friends. It is all about being one of the group.

Another important area of shopping to belong is found in the use of communication on the Internet. The big hit among teens is a product called ICQ ("I seek you") that allows whole groups of teens to chat online. ICQ is the most popular Internet messaging system. It is a huge hit. Estimates put the number of teen users at 80 million worldwide. ICQ allows teens to chat with their friends. There is no limit to the number of people that can join in. Everyone types dialogue that everyone else can read. It is like a conference call except everyone is typing. New people can join in at any time and other users can drop out when they have had enough. It is a virtual party online with everyone getting together, every night, to talk. As Jim Jamieson (Southam Newspapers) reports from an interview with Amanda, an ICQ user,

What's good about it is that everyone's there at the same time, unlike the phone where it's just you and someone else. Everybody's talking with each other about what they're doing and what's going on the rest of the day. I used to talk more on the phone, but now that this is here, I find it a whole lot easier.

Those in the business of television and radio should be worried about the Internet and about programs like ICQ. Studies show that more teens than ever are spending more time online. How does it work? How does the Internet pay for itself? It is just like television and radio. Broadcasters put out a television or radio signal for free in the hope that viewers or listeners will partake of the advertisements that accompany the content. In effect, the advertisers pay for the medium. The Internet now works in the same way. Programs like ICQ are accompanied by advertising. This not only helps to defray the costs of providing the program but also provides the producers with a profit. It is just as important today to advertise on the Internet as it used to be on television and radio. Eighty million ICQ users, for example, represent a big audience.

Food is the other big area where the teen demographic spends its own money. When it comes to food, the limited teen budget should be an overriding concern of retailers. Teens have a very limited disposable income and so like to get good value when it comes to buying food and beverages. This explains the natural affinity between teens and fast food. Fast food outlets provide the optimum combination of quantity, quality and price when it comes to serving food and so they win the teen dollar away from sit-down restaurants that have higher overhead costs. Teens care little about ambiance or atmosphere – all they want is a good quality, filling meal, at a reasonable price. They spend their limited food budget wisely, and gimmicks and promotions have little influence on their decisions on where to spend their food dollar.

Big Ticket Items – Cars, Audio Systems, Computers

Most manufacturers of big-ticket items like cars, audio systems, and computers do not target their marketing to the fourteen to sixteen-year old demographic. The assumption is that older buyers who have more cash on hand purchase such items. Nothing could be farther from the truth. Although fourteen-year olds may not have a lot of cash on hand they do have an enormous say over major family purchases. Cars, audio systems and computers get bought *for* sixteen-year olds and they usually play a big part in the decision-making process. Manufacturers and advertisers should not ignore younger demographic groups. These are important shoppers and they play a significant role in deciding how household dollars get spent.

When big-ticket items are purchased, the decision often becomes a 'collective' one that is undertaken by the entire family. What car to buy, what options to get, or what computer to purchase and what extras to buy, are often the subjects of family discussion. Usually teens will have very definitive opinions on such products and more often than not their parents, who are anxious to please, will take into account teen feelings. For example, in the decision to purchase a family computer, teens may insist that a CD 'burner' be included as an option, or in the purchase of a car they may desire a CD player. Parents pay attention to such demands and they become a central part of the decision-making process. The opinions of teens are often highly regarded by parents when it comes to certain products.

In addition there is the process of gift giving of big-ticket items. Suppose a teen wants a new audio system. Most parents are reluctant to make such a purchase on their own. They usually consult the intended gift recipient about the brand and features wanted. The shopping trip may even be a joint one where both parent and teen participate in the decision. Marketing efforts should therefore often be targeted to a younger demographic than they usually are. Young teens often play a central role in the purchase of big-ticket items.

At first glance, it may seem that teens do not buy a lot of things. The scope of the teen market is traditionally seen to be limited to clothes, food and entertainment. Retailers accept this line of thought at their risk however. The children of the baby boomers have far greater access to their parent's cash than any generation before them. As a consequence they are in the market for higher end items than most analysts give them credit for. Teens are not only buying audio systems, portable music systems, televisions and other electronics, they are also shopping in a big way for computer supplies. It is crucial to remember that this is the first generation to be raised on computers, and on the Internet, and as a result many teens are much savvier than adults when it comes to shopping for the latest computer technologies.

Teens are also big spenders in other ways. For many people, gone are the days when the family purchased on old car for a teenager. Nowadays many teens get brand new cars, fresh off the showroom floors. The wealthy baby boomers like to earn recognition, and nothing is too good for their children. Those children are not going to have to drive an old wreck like Dad did. The mid-career boomer can afford the best for his children.

The children of the later-born baby boomers are now entering the marketplace in huge numbers and the dollar value of this segment of shoppers is not insignificant. Retailers and entrepreneurs of all kinds are responding. Teens make up a significant percent of the shopping demo-graphic and their spending power is on par with just about any other segment of the market. Retailers respect this important group. Brand loyalty is important. These teens will soon be acquiring credit cards and shopping as adults. It is essential to earn their patronage.

Chapter 6

The Young Single Demographic: Shopping for Self-Esteem

The young teenager quickly grows up and becomes the young adult shopper. This group represents another demographic that is worth paying attention to. As teens enter the years of young adulthood, many enter the workforce and so they become a major shopping force. They are young, mobile, educated and more importantly, for the first time in their lives, they have disposable income. What are some of the things that the young adult shopping demographic targets its purchases toward? What are the ways in which this group shops?

A Unique Demographic

The young single demographic is unique. Here is a generation that has time to shop, extra recreational time on its hands and, usually, some surplus income. Moreover, this generation has more freedom than any other demographic group. They have more independence; they have no children, no mortgage, and few other responsibilities. They are free to do what they want, when they want. They answer to no one. This group has an untapped marketing potential that is just waiting to be exploited. But marketers, retailers, advertisers and manufacturers have yet to appreciate the demographically unique nature of this group. When it comes to demographic targeting, the young single demographic has singular characteristics that set it apart from any other.

This is a huge demographic slice that is flush with cash and one that is anxiously looking for ways to define itself through shopping. The young single demographic shops for self-esteem. They have already met their needs for belongingness and they are not yet truly at the level of shopping to self-actualize. Rather they shop to fulfill feelings of self-worth and to earn the recognition and respect of their peers. They are first-time shoppers when it comes to freedom. When they were in their teen years they only had the money to buy clothes and a few other sundries. Now, for the first time in their lives, they have a surfeit of cash that they are ready to spend. No saving for them. They are looking to spend the income from their new employment and they are eager to find shopping opportunities.

When it comes to shopping, this young unmarried group still has the dreams and aspirations of high school. They still lust after large, loud sound systems and sporty cars. But they have not yet had the time to develop shopping needs that fit with their new affluence.

The young single demographic represents an underserved group. These young shoppers have plenty of disposable income but are at a loss as to what to buy. What are some of the ways in which retailers, manufacturers and advertisers can address themselves to serving the unsatisfied needs of this group?

Fashion Shock

One of the most difficult challenges for the young single demographic is trying to stay in style. They are suddenly cut off from the information networks that exist in high school and find it challenging to keep up with the latest trends in fashion. This *fashion shock* is one of the biggest things that can occur to the high school graduate. Suddenly they seem at a loss when it comes to 'cool'. They are unsure of what to wear. Do they copy other twenty-somethings when it comes to buying clothes or should they emulate the thirteen-year olds that they see? What they find when they look in the stores is that the clothes on display are geared for teenagers. Even at the tender age of twenty, the young single demographic finds that it has started to age beyond the 'cool' teen years.

Consider a case in point. There was a trend among young teen girls to buy small purses with long straps and then to wear that strap over the shoulder and across the chest. The look created was almost military. The fashion question we can ask is whether it is appropriate for the twenty-year old to wear her purse in this same 'teen' style? And what about the twenty-two-year old or the twenty-five-year old? At what point does the young single abandon the styles that are pursued by thirteen-year olds? And better yet, with what does she replace them? As another example, consider the baggy jeans that teen boys wear. Ask yourself how a mid-twenties-something guy would look in these same jeans? Would he look silly? Would he look like he wants to be a teenager? The answer is a clear yes. But what kind of jeans is this young guy supposed to wear if he does not wear the baggy ones? The answer is that there is a *shopping gap* when it comes to the young single demographic.

Fashion shock hits both males and females as they enter their twenties and it hits them hard. What was so easy in high school suddenly becomes a major struggle. Why? Because the stores are full of 'old people' clothes. There are fashions for the young and there are fashions for the old, but seldom is there something for the young twenty-something. They start to feel awkward with teen styles but they are not yet ready for 'old people' clothes. What are they to do? The answer is that they freeze.

Frozen in Fashion

Frozen in fashion refers to the idea that the young, single adult shopper never outgrows the fashions with which they left high school. Being at a loss with what to wear, young adults cling to the fashions that were in vogue the day they graduated high school. They become stuck on these fashions and continue to wear them for years after they graduate. Just take a look around as you walk the streets and you will see twenty-year olds wearing the same clothes they wore in high school. They do not know what else to do.

Thus many people deal with the transition to adult clothing by becoming *frozen in fashion.* If the astute observer looks at what young adults wear they will quite often see a consistent pattern. Most young adult and middle-aged people have a tendency to wear the same kinds of styles that they wore as teens, into adulthood. It is almost as if time stands still in regard to the fashion consciousness of people. If there was a style of clothing that was popular as they turned the corner from the teenage years to adulthood they will tend to cling to that style as they quickly lose touch with the newly evolving teen world of fashion. Just take a look at people, men and women, and you will often see clothing and hair that reflects the day they turned twenty-one. When the time for the transition comes, they cannot bear to shift to 'old people' clothes and they cannot keep up with the new teen fashions. So they wear what they were comfortable with in their youth and they stick with it.

Retailers need to invent clothes for these people who are out of date, and advertisers need to convince them that their fashions are stuck in time. But people are stubborn when it comes to how they dress. If they are comfortable with a look, even if it is out of style, they will tend to cling to it. Nevertheless, this demographic presents a huge potential market, and a marketing challenge to the retail industry. What the business needs to do is to create new styles and fashions that are marketed explicitly to the twenty-year old demographic. They are in search of 'cool' clothes and they have the disposable income needed to make them significant shoppers. What they need are the right products to buy. They need clothes and accessories that are geared explicitly to them, rather than to thirteen-year olds. The networking of high school is gone for this group. Advertisers need to target them especially hard. It is not difficult to imagine advertising campaigns focused on the idea that twenty-somethings need to grow up.

Cars

Twenty-somethings also need guidance when it comes to things other than clothes. Retailers need to *create* demand when it comes time to sell to this significant generation. When it comes to automobiles this would appear to be an easy group to target. Young adult shoppers still lust after the cars they could only dream of as teenagers. They want sporty, 'cool' looking cars. The problem is that there is a vast difference between the sexes as to what they want. For the young women it is all about looks and style, whereas for the young men the issue is power and performance. Manufacturers are faced with these two extremes when it comes to designing their products. They can produce a stylish car that will appeal to female shoppers or they can produce a car that is noted for its high performance for male shoppers.

   It is very difficult to achieve success with a product that simultaneously appeals to both sexes. Guys call cute cars 'girl cars' and they are loath to buy them. The *Ford Focus* is a good example of a car that is considered by guys to be designed for females. For the males a high performance car like the *Integra* is the one that fits the bill. Manufacturers also have a hard time with the males of this group because usually true high performance means high price, while this demographic is also looking for value. The usual compromise is to try to achieve the production of a product that is stylish and sporty while at the same time creating an image that the car is also 'powerful' for its class. The *Pontiac Sunfire* is an excellent example of a sporty car that is designed to appeal to both sexes.

   What can retailers do to make cars more appealing to the young single demographic? What kinds of features is this group looking for? Clearly any attempt to appeal to their practical side is doomed to failure. For example, it might be pointed out to them that in just a couple of years they are likely to get married and so they may want to buy a more practical vehicle such as a sedan, rather than a sports car. Such an appeal will fall on deaf ears, as this group is not forward looking in its outlook. They live for the present and cannot imagine the idea of buying a four-door sedan when they are young and unattached. This example provides an excellent illustration of the mentality of the young single demographic. They live for the moment, and practicality is usually the farthest thing from their mind.

The truth of the matter is that a vehicle needs to appeal to the young single demographic at its face value. It has to appeal here and now, with no attention to the future. Manufacturers need to design vehicles that appeal to a demographic that is interested in shopping for the present. These shoppers want a car that makes them feel good. It has to be youthful, stylish and have the air of a sports car.

Sports cars have been on the market for many years now. It is a difficult concept to get a handle on, but most people know intuitively what it means. A short wheelbase, aerodynamic styling, large wheels, two doors and a certain 'look' are the principal features of the classic sports car. Manufacturers can design these features into almost any car but it also has to be on the small side for it truly to be viewed as a sports car. *Chrysler*, for instance, has designed most of these features into its *Intrepid* but, because it is a large car, it is still perceived by younger buyers as an 'old people' car.

What other features of a vehicle will appeal to the young single demographic? It should probably engage their sense of mobility and adventure. A vehicle that calls on their sense of personal freedom will probably be a success. Some manufacturers are attempting to branch out beyond the sports car theme into off-road vehicles for this demographic. The *Pontiac Aztec* is a good example of an 'off road' style of vehicle that appeals to the adventuresome nature of the twenty-something group. The back of the vehicle has an attachable tent for camping. The success of this groundbreaking vehicle will probably set the tone for other manufacturers to follow. A good illustration of *Pontiac*'s attempt to appeal to a younger demographic with this vehicle was shown by the fact that one was given away to the winner of the popular television series *Survivor*.

Young adult shoppers are shopping for self-esteem. They want a vehicle that makes them feel good about themselves and also one that will impress their friends. Driving a 'cool' car is a badge of honor among social circles and an appropriate car will be noted and, doted over, by acquaintances. Shopping for a car for the young single demographic is shopping at the fourth level. This includes needs for self-respect, the respect of others and prestige. Manufacturers, retailers and advertisers should pay close attention to this shopper's need for self-esteem. What is really important is how the car makes the buyer feel about himself in the eyes of his friends. This is truly the bottom line in car sales for the twenty-something group. They want a car that makes an impression with the other people in their lives, whether it is friends or family. A car makes a statement about its owner; it says, "This is who I am". It has to be 'cool', sporty, and illustrative of a carefree and adventuresome social life. It is like a trip to Europe. The same kind of person that takes a carefree trip through Europe will want a car that conveys a sense of the carefree personality and attitude of the participant. The car is a means to an end; it makes the person in the eyes of others.

Travel

A big retail area that is going unexploited by businesses is in the international travel of the young single demographic. Travel agencies seem to devote most of their efforts to wooing the baby boom generation, when there is a whole group of twenty-somethings that is ready and anxious to travel. Just ask yourself how often you have seen an ad for travel that is targeted at this demographic. Instead the agencies target older age groups and families as the ones that are seen as ready to travel. Carry out a survey of older teens and twenty-year olds, however, and you will find that almost all of them have plans to travel, or at least they dream of travel. Favorite destinations are Europe and Australia, and it is seen to be 'cool' to talk about your future travel plans. Those who have already traveled carry it around like a badge of honor. They get the bragging rights and get to talk among their friends of their adventures. Travel has become a huge area of interest among the young single demographic, and travel agencies and airlines can direct their efforts at selling trips to this generation.

Imagine a car buyer's package that includes free airfare to Europe. Is this an effective way to sell a carefree, sporty car to the young single demographic? It certainly would seem to be. Right now car dealers offer buying incentives, in the form of discounts, to college graduates. A much more effective path for this generation would be to offer them free airfare to Australia with the purchase of the car that is targeted to their demographic. Clearly such a marketing package would be an attractive one to a generation that is ready to explore the world, whether it is in their new car or on an international trip.

Buying a trip is shopping at the fourth level. It is about self-esteem and about the image that one portrays to friends and the rest of the world. The trip is not about seeing the sights; it is about expressing the self and creating an image of the self. Shopping to meet esteem needs is important. Self-esteem comes from the way we are reflected in the eyes of others. A large part of that reflection is determined by the possessions we own and the activities we perform. Travel is about defining the self. It sends a message to others about the traveler's personality. It is an extension of the self, in the same way that clothing and cars are, and it should be marketed as such. Travel agencies, airlines, and other businesses can get a lot more mileage out of the marketing of travel to the young single demographic.

Entertainment

One of the biggest areas to which the young single demographic will direct its expenditures is with respect to entertainment. Having none of the responsibilities of married life, this group has surplus time on its hands in a big way and so is looking to spend its hard-earned cash on ways to fill the voids of single life. Movies are big. This group is one of the most important ones to the movie going demographic. Although they are still willing to take in the occasional teen movie, their tastes have become more sophisticated than that. They want high quality, engaging movies that appeal to their age group. It is a difficult demographic to please; they are young and impatient and anything less than top notch will not garner their attention.

For movie producers it is important to remember that this demographic is unique. It is close enough to the teen years to have the teen attitude but is not yet old enough to have the responsibilities of adulthood. This group will want a product that reinforces its own self-image of a carefree and adventurous lifestyle that is combined with the cavalier attitude of youth. Movies for this demographic need to play upon the idea that life is just for fun and that it is too early to worry about the pressures of adulthood and parenthood. Good times and freedom are the order of the day.

Television bores this group. They see it as a medium targeted to young kids and older adults, that is, to families. The young single demographic has better things to do with its time than watch television. When they have free time they want to go *out* and they despise the idea of just sitting home. Their adventuresome lifestyle does not have room in it for sitting in front of the television when there are more exciting things to do. For advertisers this disinterest in television by the twenty-something demographic presents a real challenge. It means it is difficult to reach this group through traditional television advertising. Other sources of exposure need to be found because this group just does not watch television.

Radio is where the young single demographic spends its time. They aspire to be attuned to music like they were in their teen years and they spend a lot of time listening to the radio. For the advertiser who wants to get a message across to this demographic group, radio is the medium of choice. Try as they might, however, this demographic just cannot keep up with the times. Gone are the days when it was possible to keep up with all the new groups and songs. As the young single demographic loses the networking of high school, so too it loses its ability to stay 'cool'. In the same way that this group is frozen in fashion, so it is frozen in music. It is at this age that people start to lose touch with the latest trends and fads. Instead they start to fall back on the music they knew in high school as their primary source of entertainment. If you do not believe this, just ask yourself why so many radio stations continue to play songs from the sixties and seventies. Clearly this music is targeted to the baby boomers that *still* listen to the same songs they did when they were in high school. For the producers of radio the young single demographic represents a difficult group. They want to hear new songs but they also want to hear those songs they were familiar with just a few years ago. Radio promoters need to decide which demographic, teen or young adult, they are targeting. There is a subtle difference between them.

Night Clubs and Bars

When it comes to nightclubs and bars, the young single demographic hits its zenith. Free of the responsibilities of adulthood and parenthood, this demographic group is free to spend its time and its money on nightly get-togethers. The bar takes the place of the television for the twenty-something demographic. They have a strong need to socialize and get together with friends and acquaintances. This is where the young single demographic fulfills its need for *belongingness*. By socializing with a circle of friends they create the feeling of being members of a group. They have no husbands or wives so the need to belong to a social group is a strong one. Ties to their immediate family – Moms, Dads, brothers and sisters – are slowly being cut. For a few years, then, the social group takes the place of the family for this demographic.

Choosing to participate at a particular club or bar is a form of shopping. One 'buys' the services of one establishment over another. What kind of facility does the young single shop for? The number one requirement is that there must be a consensus that all members of the social group will participate at the same locations. This is crucial to the sense of belonging. There may be more than one establishment that is popular among a group but all that matters are that friends be found at whatever place is chosen. Members of such social circles will never go to a new club without the agreement of at least some of the group. What is the point of going to a bar if none of your friends are there? People like to feel that they fit in with their friends or peers, and so choosing an establishment to achieve a sense that one belongs to a group is very important.

For the owners of such establishments the key is to become popular among circles of friends. This can be difficult to achieve. Very often new clubs become all the rage for a short while but then lose their luster as their popularity fades. At the same time some clubs seem to be able to hold their clientele regardless of fads and so, in the long run, it is these places that succeed. What is the secret to their success? It is in their ability to attract *new* circles of friends as more senior ones age and drop out of the bar scene. This can be accomplished by having a reputation as a place where friends get together and by offering incentives to keep loyal customers coming back. But the process mainly works through the reputation of the place. This is a difficult thing to get a handle on, but some clubs or bars are able to earn and maintain a strong reputation as 'the place to be' even as their clientele changes throughout the years.

What about the choices of these shoppers when it comes to the products inside the bars? Clearly the biggest area of competition is found in the 'beer wars' as rival companies seek to attract loyal clients. Brand loyalty and brand choice are obviously the subjects of much research done by beer companies. How *do* you get that twenty-one-year old guy to say *Bud* when he is asked what kind of beer he wants? Here again there would appear to have to be a social consensus among any given group as to what is 'cool' and what is not when it comes to brand names. One thing is certain. Young beer drinkers will want their own brands. They will not want to order the same beer that their Dad drinks. It is important for them to show their independence and it is important to become your own person – to establish your own identity – when it comes to product choice. Advertisers can emphasize this dimension of the product when it comes to selling beer. More importantly, when it comes to advertising it is crucial to appeal to the young single demographics need to belong. The choice of a brand of beer should reinforce and further define one's membership in the group. Typically this involves choosing the most popular products, or at least the most popular among the group. In addition, in many circumstances members of this demographic will also choose exotic products, such as the Mexican beer *Corona*, to demonstrate their worldliness and adventuresome nature. In either case the choice is made in the context of the social group and is part of the group dynamic.

Shopping for products and choosing places to go to is a way of demonstrating one's membership in a group. As the responsibilities of matrimony and parenthood come to the fore, the nightclubbing lifestyle will soon be left behind. The members of this demographic are only active participants for a few years. In most cases, marriage soon leads to a radical change of lifestyle.

Lifestyle Gear

Another area where the young single demographic is likely to have high demands is with respect to what we might call lifestyle gear. This would include items like high-end sports gear, sunglasses, athletic shoes and hikers, hiking equipment, mountain bikes, camping equipment and so on. In such areas, branding is of extreme importance to this group. They really will not deal with products that do not have brand names.

This is a generation that has been raised to believe that the only products worth having are those with well-known brand names. This emphasis on branding is a part of the cycle of belongingness. Knowing what brands are 'cool' and are high quality is part of being a member of the 'in' crowd. As a consequence, branding takes on a much broader significance than retailers and manufacturers would suspect.

For the employed, twenty-something demographic there exists the possibility of buying all of that lifestyle gear that one could only dream about in high school. Having new found disposable income, this group is ready to buy gear and equipment that helps it to define itself. The demographic likes to see itself as outdoor and health oriented with an active lifestyle. The same self-concept applies to this group whether it is buying cars, skiing equipment or beer. They like to see themselves as skiers, snowboarders, hikers and bikers. And even if they are not fit or active they still know what brands of snowboards and bikes are 'cool'. There is a unique mentality to their age group and smart advertisers should devote themselves to satisfying these self-images when they promote their products. This group has a strong demand for a whole line of lifestyle gear that is often going unmet. This represents an area where there is great retail potential for those who understand the mindset of the young single demographic.

There is also a hefty dose of self-esteem that goes along with lifestyle gear for the twenty-something group. The group is anxious to create an image that is typically portrayed in beer commercials; the young, single, good-looking sociable lifestyle that has lots of friends, lots of good times, and little or no responsibilities. Life *is* a beer commercial. For the purposes of self-esteem, it is important to own the right lifestyle gear or at least to be aware of the trendiest products. Whether it is snowboards, water skis, and snow skis or backpacks and boots, it is important to be up-to-date on the latest products. Self-esteem, and feelings of self-worth and confidence, are associated with this generation's lifestyle gear and self-image.

Fitness Centers

Another area where the young single demographic presents a solid source of demand is with respect to fitness centers. These are usually targeted to this demographic and indeed this group represents the bread and butter of the industry. Young adults want to go to fitness centers not only to work out, but to be seen, to meet friends and to socialize. Those in the industry should take pains to ensure that the primary purpose of a visit to a fitness center is social, while the secondary purpose is fitness.

It would seem that there is demand in this area that is not being fulfilled. It is suspected that more customers could be encouraged to visit fitness centers if more stress was placed on the social aspect. Visiting a fitness center should be as easy as visiting a bar and perhaps there is more demand for 'lower level' types of fitness centers where there is more emphasis on simple and non-strenuous kinds of activity in which anyone can participate. Examples of such activities might include indoor archery, indoor golf, or beach volleyball, where there is more emphasis on fun and less on vigorous exercise. A big stumbling block to many current fitness centers is that many potential customers see the activities as too strenuous. No doubt many potential customers are also turned off by the thought of having to change clothing and even shower in front of strangers. Fitness centers could easily overcome this obstacle by appropriate design of facilities wherein the privacy of patrons is guaranteed.

A recent trend in the fitness center industry has been toward same sex centers, particularly for women. Clearly these are intended for patrons who are more serious about exercise and less serious about socializing, although even in these cases same sex socializing remains an important consideration.

Regardless of the focus of a fitness center its greatest source of advertising is word of mouth. Friends invite friends to fitness centers and most operators are very aware of this dimension of the business. In fact, it is very common to see promotional efforts where a patron earns a discount by attracting acquaintances to a center. Free, limited time memberships are also a common strategy, where the expectation is that a client can be attracted to the business for the long term if they are just given a start.

In any case, the young single adult demographic is always searching for things to do, especially with friends, and there seems to be unlimited demand for more innovative approaches to the fitness center industry.

Generational Transference

There are other areas where the young single demographic presents opportunities to retailers that are going unexploited. It is important to remember that these are, in many cases, first-time shoppers. Consider that they may be young adults who have moved away from home for the first time and so they are faced with purchasing decisions that they have never faced before. They have to buy things now that were only purchased before by their parents. As a consequence, this group presents some unique marketing challenges.

One implication is that the single, twenty-something demographic will be shopping at the first and second levels for the first time in their lives. They will be purchasing some of the essentials of life and some basic necessities. Shopping at the first level implies that they will be purchasing elementary physical needs such as food, clothing and shelter. Shopping at the second level implies shopping for security needs including items that are essential to health and safety. Consider the implications. For the first time in their life the young, single shopper may be buying something like safety razors on their own. Such a seemingly simple buying decision actually raises a host of complex marketing questions. Does the young shopper have a brand preference? Has advertising swayed them? Do they buy the same brand that their parents bought? There are a lot of interesting questions to be answered.

Shopping for physical survival needs includes basic foodstuffs and essential clothing. Even at this level competing companies fight diligently to put their brand in the forefront. Consider the young adult shopper buying everyday products such as canned soup, TV dinners or instant coffee. The question that can be asked is to what extent marketers are aware of this important demographic and to what extent do they target it. How often do you see ads for such products that are directed to twenty-year olds? The answer would be rarely, if ever. Advertisers tend to target older demographics for such products even though once brand preference is established it is hard to change. The time to grab these shoppers is when they *first* set out to buy branded products. If you can capture their attention on the first purchase, they are likely to become brand loyal for life.

The *generational transference* of brand preference is also important. Young shoppers tend to buy the brands that their parents buy and so brand loyalty transfers from generation to generation. If Mom buys *Tide* laundry detergent or *Campbell's* soup, so too will her daughter tend to buy the same brands. Retailers and advertisers can break the cycle of generational transfer by appealing to the psyche of the young adult shopper. It is necessary to break the mold, to establish in the mind of the young shopper that he or she wants to be different from Mom and Dad and wants to make his or her own purchasing decisions. Some automobile advertisers follow this tact when they say "Not your Dad's car". The same logic can be applied to all manner of products – especially foodstuffs – that the young single demographic buys. This generation is ripe for advertising that conveys a message that it is time to make your own decisions and it is time to choose products that are different from those your parents bought. If *Levi's* are "the jeans your parents wore" then *Tide* should be "the laundry detergent that your Mother used".

Shopping for basic foodstuffs and essential clothing is the shopping that everyone must do to survive. Even the young twenty-something generation has a need for bread and milk, and socks and underwear. These are essentials for which everyone must shop. Shopping for physical survival needs is an important element of the shopping equation. Although it may seem dull and unexciting, to the retailers of such products it is a life and death struggle for market share. Witness the extent to which elementary products like underwear, lingerie, soups, sauces and even gum are advertised. It is all about getting that consumer to pick up that product at the moment of decision. The young single demographic is one that should be targeted more forcefully than it is. It is important to remember that they are first-time shoppers.

When it comes to the second level of shopping – for health and security needs – there is little to distinguish it from the first level. Once again you have first-time shoppers shopping for essentials of health and safety – such as toothbrushes, deodorant, and razors – and their minds are open to new brand preferences if the mold of intergenerational transfer can be broken. And even though these are 'routine' purchases, they form a significant part of the shopping dollar.

There is another area where the significance of the young single demographic should not be overlooked. The single young adult represents an enigma to the retailer. What do you sell to a twenty-five year old? The answer is that there exists with this demographic an opportunity to create new demand. What is needed is to get this shopper beyond the aspirations of high school and into a new realm of shopping. Retailers and manufacturers need to invent marketing strategies that will make single young adults strive to buy more adult products. Since most of these young singles rent their accommodations, an obvious marketing opportunity is in the home furnishings and appliances markets. When was the last time you saw a furniture ad that was targeted to young singles in apartments? When was the last time you saw home appliances, or even cleaning products, marketed to the young single demographic? This is a huge segment of the market that is destined to become ever more important as the children of the baby boomers age. The advertising message needs to be conveyed to this demographic that it is growing up and needs to spend its money on things other than adolescent fantasies.

The young single group is an interesting demographic that has time to shop, money to buy, but a very limited selection of merchandise in which it is interested. This is the stage at which young adult shoppers are able to buy all of the things they longed for as teenagers. Thus there is a demand for things like expensive audio equipment (for the home and car), sporty cars, short adventure-style trips, high-end sports gear, expensive jewelry, and more and better clothing and accessories. This is the shopper with a fairly large amount of disposable income that is not yet ready to make the big purchases – homes, furniture, boats, cottages, life insurance – that adults make. This demographic probably represents one of the most under-served shopping groups that exist. These shoppers have disposable income and plenty of time to shop, but the number of items available for purchase is limited largely to the dreams of high school. They are anxious to define themselves as young adults, but beyond items such as those listed above, and especially the sporty car, they are very limited in the range of items they wish to buy. As an illustration of this idea, consider the range of merchandise available in a store like *Wal-Mart*, and ask how much of that merchandise is of interest to the nineteen to twenty-nine year old, unmarried demographic. The answer is that there is little that a single twenty-five year old wants to buy in *Wal-Mart*.

Chapter 7

The Young Married Demographic: Shopping as Grown-Ups

It does not take long before the single, young adults discussed in the last chapter undergo a metamorphosis. The laws of demographics dictate that after a few short years of the single life they will be ready to get married. What happens to the young single demographic as it undergoes this change? How do its patterns of consumption change? We shall see that the answer is that the biggest lifetime revolution in shopping patterns occurs at this stage. When twenty-somethings get married they undergo an enormous upheaval in their style of buying. There is nothing else quite like it in the evolution of shopping. In particular, the young married demographic undergoes a shift in how they shop and why they shop. For demographic targeters there is a fundamental shift required in the perception of this group. Marriage bells change everything and the wise retailer will have to reset his sights if he wants to keep pace with the radical changes that this group undergoes.

They will be buying their first house. They will be renovating and decorating that house and they will be buying all of the equipment and furnishings that a first house requires. They will be at the age to first start buying mutual funds, life insurance, house insurance and all of the other sundries that go along with adulthood. In addition, this generation is still young enough to want to stay in style, and so they will be active participants in the clothing and accessory markets. Their youthfulness also implies that they still go out and so will partake of the food, entertainment and related industries. Take a look at the myriad of products of which this group is in need:

- Lawnmowers, garden tools, high-pressure pumps, hoses, spreaders, trimmers, etc
- Living room furniture, dining room furniture, end tables, lamps, accessories, paintings
- Washing machine, stove, fridge, washer, dryer, dishwasher, microwave
- Television, sound system, VCR, satellite system, DVD player, computer, video camera

- Beds, dressers, nightstands, lamps, desk
- Dishes, pots and pans, linens, bedding, towels
- Curtains and blinds
- Fencing, driveway, sod, sprinklers, trees and shrubs, patio, decking.

The list is impressive, and there are many more small things (tools, sewing machines) that have not been added. In short, the job of setting up a household for the first time is a formidable task and is clearly one that requires a great deal of shopping. The young married demographic represents the champion shoppers of them all by virtue of the huge amount of things that are part of the typical married life.

An important characteristic of the young married demographic is that, as a shopping unit, it is young and impressionable. Although this group starts on average at about twenty-five years of age, when it comes to shopping for most of the things in life, this group consists of beginners. They have never purchased 'grown-up' products before and so are likely to be novices when it comes to many of the purchases that they make. Significantly, they are also new to many of the adult brand names on products and so they are likely to be easily swayed to new names and products. Consider products like lawnmowers, air conditioners or fridges and stoves. Such products represent a whole new world of shopping to the young married demographic and so they are wide open to new brand names and new promotions.

Like other shoppers, the young married demographic is concerned with more than just acquiring goods and services when they shop. They are also concerned with fulfilling emotional and psychological needs when they buy things. Buying the basics for a household is a first-time experience and so this shopping takes place at a higher level than it might for other, older shoppers. While buying a washing machine may be routine and dull for the older shopper, for the young married demographic it may represent a higher level of shopping because it is a first-time experience. This kind of shopping can be challenging and rewarding for this demographic group. It involves comparison shopping, shopping for price and quality and shopping for features on the items purchased. Part of the motivation for this demographic is shopping to belong. They buy the items that their peers buy, in order to fulfill their need to fit in with friends and relatives. If everyone you know has a video camera, you will want to get one too. This is a way for retailers and advertisers to appeal to this demographic group – by using peer pressure as a motivator. 'Keeping up with the Joneses' is an important concept at this age of shopping. The young married demographic also shops at the fourth level – to achieve feelings of self-esteem. Owning the right products, the right house, the right vehicle, and so on is part of feeling a sense of self-worth and esteem in the eyes of their peers. Shopping at the fifth level is somewhat beyond the needs of the young married demographic. Most of their purchases are about practical need and necessity.

The Young Married – Pulled in Different Directions

As we saw, consumption in the young *single* life is often limited to the dreams of high school. Sporty cars and big sound systems are often the only things that the young single group sets its sights on. Not so with the young married. Suddenly a whole new world of shopping opens up and the possibilities for buying products are almost endless. The twenty to thirty-year old married demographic has its sights set on all of the things that are part of an adult life. Interestingly, they also have their hearts set on acquiring some of the dreams of their youth.

The young married demographic lives a life full of contradictions. They have activities ongoing in a number of directions simultaneously. For one thing they are busy with their careers. It is an exciting time of transfers, advancements, promotions and achieving job security. Working hard and working long hours is one of their main priorities in life. At the same time they are still young, have single friends, and so they also try to live the social life that they did before they got married. They are not quite ready to abandon entirely the young single lifestyle. Nevertheless they are also married and so with marriage comes new responsibilities and demands on their time. They are expected to start to act like adults in their leisure and social activities. Living the partying life of the young single group starts to be frowned upon by friends and relatives. In addition, this group is expected to have children and so there are certain hopes raised in that regard. In short, the young married demographic is pulled in a number of different directions all at once and their lives are hectic and sometimes confusing and self-contradictory. For example, they may be buying their first new car and so still want the sports car they have longed after for years. Now that they have a job and an income their dreams can come true. But at the same time they know they will be having children in just a couple of years and so a practical family sedan seems like a more sensible option. The young married demographic is often torn with shopping decisions of this sort and it only adds to the difficulties of this confusing time of life.

Retailers need to help the young married demographic sort out these complexities. They need to offer products that simultaneously satisfy the desires of youth with the responsibilities of adulthood. This is a daunting task. With an automobile the solution is clear – the young married need a sporty car that will also double as a practical family car. But with many other products the answer is not so obvious. Clothes, furnishings, groceries, and home appliances are just some of the types of products for which there is no easy solution. The challenge to the retailer is to satisfy the youthfulness of this group while at the same time providing the everyday necessities of life. This calls for products that *mix* these two extremes together; clothes that are at once youthful but mature or furnishings that are simultaneously appealing to the two personalities of the young married demographic.

It is difficult to identify examples of advertising strategies that have been targeted to the dual personalities of the young married. Ads seem to play to the youth of this market segment (for example, sporty cars), and little attention is paid to the practical needs of this demographic. This approach represents a failed marketing strategy inasmuch as this maturing demographic also needs to see a practical side to its purchases. Advertising campaigns should address this imbalance and should appeal to the adult side of this demographic.

Designer Label Targeting

There is another way to appeal to the split personality of the young married demographic. It is important to remember that this is a generation that has grown up with product branding and designer labels as a mainstream part of product choice.

The young married demographic is overlooked as a source of interest with respect to brand names. Most of the products that are of interest to the young married demographic – such as furniture, appliances, and home furnishings – are sold without using designer labels. This sales strategy represents an enormous gap in modern marketing. Many more of the products of interest to the young married group could be marketed with brand names or designer labels. The *Tommy Hilfiger* group has undertaken one excellent example of such a marketing strategy. This company is now selling sheet sets and bedroom coordinates under its well-known name. In addition, they are selling hosiery and jewelry under the *Tommy* name. This marketing strategy successfully targets the brand name to the demographic group *as it ages*. As a consequence, as the teens that grew up with *Tommy* become older, adult products are available to them with the same *Tommy* name. This is a demographic targeting approach that many other companies could follow. More and more, products for the young married should be identified with the designer labels of the demographics youth. One can imagine furniture, linens, dishes, and many other home furnishings being sold under the umbrella of designer labels.

This is not *Martha Stewart*. The twenty-somethings regard such labels as being for older people and such product lines are not attractive to them. The same goes for the other 'in-house' fashion lines that many retailers try to use on household items. The young married demographic needs to see the designer labels of their youth. These are familiar to them and these are what they are comfortable with. As they pass out of the teen and young adult years they start to fall back on the brands they knew when they were young and 'cool', and retailers and manufacturers can provide them with such labels.

Unprecedented Demand

The married twenty-somethings represent one of the most important demographic groups. They represent a source of demand for products that is unprecedented. There is really only one time in life where one has to set out literally to buy *everything* associated with an adult life, and this is it. The young married demographic needs to acquire all of the products that are part of every grown-up life.

When is the last time you saw a stove and fridge combination being targeted to a young demographic? When is the last time you saw bedding and towels being actively pitched to twenty-somethings? What we see instead is a huge contradiction in marketing. Many such products seem to be targeted to the older adult demographic that, in most cases, already owns the products. If there ever was misdirection in mainstream marketing, this is it. A washer and dryer combo should be directed to the twenty-something couple that is likely to buy it. Once purchased it is likely to last many years, so it will be a long time before another demographic is interested in the product. The question is how do you make a washer and dryer, or a fridge and stove, attractive to the young married demographic? The answer is easy. If it can be done with cars, it can be done with anything. Such household items need to be marketed with the same ideas as other products. They need to be seen as being appropriate to the busy, young lifestyle of this active demographic. It is not difficult to imagine ads for basic household items that portray their owner's lifestyles as young and energetic. It is not difficult to imagine everyday products being pitched to the egos of the young married demographic.

The young married demographic represents a huge marketing potential not so much because of its size but because it is ready to purchase all of the necessities of life over a very short time span. Young couples today do not want to wait to acquire the basics like their parents did. A young married lifestyle without a dishwasher or a microwave oven is almost unimaginable to them. They want it all and they want it all at once.

The Transformation

Young married shoppers undergo a transformation of sorts. In their young single days they were obsessed with socializing and 'going out'. Once the magic of marriage hits them, however, they become different kinds of people. A crucial part of the institution of marriage is shopping together. The experience of sharing an apartment or owning a house puts a new spin on a young couple's life, and suddenly the shared experience of shopping together becomes one of the most important parts of marriage. It is a special time; a time to share thoughts, hopes, dreams and aspirations. It is an exciting time. A multitude of products is being looked at that has never before been considered by this group. Suddenly, mundane items like washers and stoves become important products to a group that previously had no interest in them whatsoever. It is a unique time of life; a time when the foundations of marriage and a life together are being built. Like it or not, shopping is a central part of this stage of life.

The young married have plenty of time to shop. Even though their lives are busy with work, they still have many leisurely hours to spend. Going out to bars and clubs has fallen by the wayside and so there are many free evenings to shop. Shopping is a form of entertainment for this group. It is easy to do and it is free. It is a good way to spend a few hours in the evening, or on the weekend, and it is a good way to share the bonds of marriage. Marketers should play to this element of the twenty-something demographic. Products, such as home decorating products, can be marketed in a way that plays to the special role it will play in the marriage. Decorating and furnishing a place to live is an important way in which couples share their lives together. This aspect of marriage represents an enormous marketing opportunity that is not being exploited to its full potential. Products should be sold for their emotional value as well as for their practical worth. Decorating a home is a very personal experience and many couples struggle to find the products that adequately represent their desires. Remember this is a group that just a few short years or even months ago was young and single. The world of marriage, and sharing product purchases, is new to them and so they need all the help they can get from marketers.

There is no doubt that very few products are marketed specifically with the young married demographic in mind. Most household products seem to be targeted at older demographic groups in spite of the fact that many of them are already saturated with all of the things they need. Who browses the paintings and wall hangings in department stores? Who is looking at lamps or bedspreads? Who is it that is most interested in beginner home audio systems or VCRs? Clearly there is a whole line of products that is of especial interest to the married twenty-somethings.

What Level does this Group Shop?

We saw previously that the teen demographic shops almost exclusively to belong. Shopping at the third level keeps teens focused on staying in style and fitting-in with their peers. The young married demographic, on the other hand, evolves beyond the need to belong. As teens transform into the twenties the need, and indeed the ability, to stay in style starts to fade. The goal of shopping becomes less important as the twenty-somethings set their sights on higher levels of the hierarchy. The next level of shopping involves the need for self-esteem and it is indeed at this level where the young married demographic focuses its efforts.

Shopping for self-esteem is a central part of the levels of shopping needs. At the age of the twenty-somethings it is important that shopping satisfy feelings for status, self-reward and for pride. For teens, self-esteem is expressed mainly through the clothes and accessories they wear, through their hairstyle, and through their music. They have little in the way of material possessions and so the expression of the inner-self is limited to these few items. With a young couple, self-esteem is expressed through their new possessions. For the first time in life they are buying all of the things that 'adults' own and so they derive a great deal of pleasure and emotional satisfaction from such belongings.

Shopping for self-esteem needs is about shopping in order to create a favorable opinion or appreciation of oneself. It is about feelings of pride, confidence and self-respect that emanate not just from the act of shopping but from owning those possessions that make one feel good about oneself in the eyes of others. Twenty-something married shoppers are building a life together and are acquiring all of life's significant belongings. They derive enormous feelings of self-satisfaction from their shopping behavior and indeed this is one of the most important times of life for the psychological rewards that shopping brings.

Retailers, manufacturers and advertisers probably underestimate the significance of this level of shopping for this group. It is a time of life like no other. For shoppers who just a few years ago were teens, even the simplest possessions take on enormous meaning. Decorating that first house or apartment is a time of pleasure and joy, and a big part of the gratification of the process comes from the fact that the place of residence is designed to be shown-off to others. Thus the self-esteem comes from the pride and self-congratulations that are reflected in the eyes of visitors. That first house or apartment is decorated not just for the self but to impress others – friends and relatives – who come to visit. It is a central part of the act of a couple defining their life together by the shared expression of their belongings. For the woman, beautiful furniture might be a high priority while for the man perhaps a home theatre system is more important. Whatever the case, the point is to be able to show-off these possessions to others as an icon of the marriage itself. This is indeed significant shopping.

As shoppers shopping at the fourth level, what is most important to the young married demographic? What are their concerns? What are they most focused on?

Home Appliances

Unlike their young, single counterparts, the young married start to get interested in what are usually seen to be mundane or everyday products. There is a reason for this. They have an essential need to acquire all of the basic household necessities. Household necessities cover a lot of territory, everything from dishes to carpeting, and purchases of such products are very important to this demographic. How can they be targeted? How can marketers better hone in on the desires and demands of this important group?

The young married demographic is looking for good quality products that will satisfy their needs but they do not want to spend a lot. One key to success with this group then is to provide them with the products they want at prices that are appropriate to the budget of a young couple that is just starting out. At the same time, they have plenty of time to shop. This is important. It means that married twenty-somethings will be serious comparison shoppers because they will have the time to compare products. For retailers, manufacturers and advertisers this is an important characteristic of this demographic. Price and product quality must be competitive although design is also an important consideration.

What is the key to success in grabbing the attention of this group? The answer seems to be found in the fact that they do not want to give up their youth. Even though they are looking at 'old people' products for the first time, they do not want the products they buy to seem old. They want carpets, washers, furniture, lamps and wall pictures that are *their own*. They do not want to buy what Mom and Dad already own. They are setting out on their own life and so they want life-defining products that are truly unique to them. This idea sets a high standard for manufacturers and advertisers who need to produce and sell products that are seen to have a new spin. This should not be too difficult a challenge because such a marketing approach has been undertaken with many other products for many years. Advertisers do their best, for example, to produce innovations in products like toothbrushes, and to sell those innovative products to the public. If it can be done with toothbrushes it can be done with anything. It is just a matter of finding the right marketing spin for each and every product that is of interest to the young married demographic.

For home appliances the right marketing spin will evolve from introducing innovations to ordinary products that make them unique from the twenty-something point of view. This may involve a minor or major change in product design. A typical example is found in the case of the washing machine. North Americans prefer top loading washers while Europeans prefer front loading styles. A potential product marketing idea is to try to sell front loaders to young couples by convincing them that it not only is unique to their generation but that it also washes better than their Mother's. This is just one simple idea. The point is to suggest that manufacturers need to take simple everyday household appliances – microwaves, crock pots, toasters, broiler ovens, and even can openers – and give them design innovations that make them interesting or different to this young demographic that is buying them for the first time.

Like other shoppers, the married twenty-somethings want products that make them feel good. When they buy a home appliance they should come away from the transaction with a sense of satisfaction and well-being. These are items to fill the new home or apartment and when you are at this stage, and age, each and every item is important.

One thing the young married are willing to put up with is a little inconvenience in order to save money. Stores like *Ikea* are a perfect example of the kind of product that appeals to this group. They are more than willing to haul bulky items home themselves and to put up with the hassle of self-assembly if it will save them a few dollars. Unlike older shoppers, who do not have the time or the inclination to assemble things themselves, the younger group is willing to put up with this inconvenience if it means a savings. This logic applies to all kinds of home furnishings that are self assembled, especially furniture. There is probably a bigger market for this type of product than manufacturers and retailers are aware of, and there is undoubtedly room for growth in this sector. Young people *enjoy* the shared experience of assembling their own furniture; it makes them feel good about their purchases and gives them a sense of accomplishment, not to mention the savings on the budget.

Cars

On the surface, it does not appear difficult to design a car that will appeal to the married twenty-somethings. They are still young and childless and a sports car will appeal to them. However, the big change comes when they have children because although they still think of themselves as young, the presence of children demands something more practical when it comes to an automobile. How are designers of automobiles to approach this difficult design problem?

One good answer comes from the designers of *General Motor's Saturn* automobile. Many readers will be aware of the unique and innovative idea that the *Saturn* engineers came up with. One of the sporty *Saturn*'s is basically a two-door coupe in style. In order to overcome the restrictions which this places on entry to the back seat, the engineers at *Saturn* added a third small door, immediately behind the driver's door that provides better access to the back seat. Thus the sporty *Saturn* coupe can also double as a car to take the kids to soccer. And that is how they advertise it. It is this kind of innovation that will sell especially to the young married demographic. It allows them to have their 'sports car' but also allows for the practical problems associated with children. This is the kind of original improvement that all manufacturers should strive towards if they are interested in the twenty-something demographic.

Saturn is an especially good example because it appeals to the twenty-something demographic that does not have a lot of money to spend on cars. Manufacturers also need to design smaller, low budget cars that are produced with the young family in mind. At the moment there seems to be an overabundance of sporty cars, and cars aimed at older demographics, while not enough attention is paid to the young married demographic. Once they have children they will be ready to trade in their sports cars for practical family vehicles that are new, stylish and different from their parents' cars. They need to be loaded with features that are designed for young children, an aspect of design that is largely ignored at present. For example, how many sedans are there that have optional cargo holders for toys in the back seat? There are a lot of simple ideas that will sell to young parents.

Entertainment

The young married demographic undergoes a profound transformation. With the advent of married life comes a profound shift in lifestyle. Probably most notable within this change is the massive shift to television watching. As young singles these people had little or no interest in television, but with marriage this all changes. This group has surplus time on its hands and the days of going to clubs and bars are long since past. Married life brings time together at home and much of this spare time is filled with television. Their formerly active lifestyle becomes a more sedentary one and there is a need to fill time with more mundane activities. Like it or not, this is the nature of marriage and adulthood. For marketers this is a time to use television to appeal to this generation. They are anxious to shop, and to buy the accoutrements of adulthood, and so they are ripe for advertising that is pointed in this direction.

The young married 'rediscover' television. They have not really watched much of it since they were adolescents. For advertisers this represents a new demographic that is watching and, although they do not have a lot of money, they are active shoppers that do have time to spend on browsing.

When it comes to radio, the young married are still active listeners but they start to lose the intensity of their teen years. Once they leave high school they quickly start to lose touch with what is 'cool' in music and suddenly their favorite songs turn out be 'classics' from the past. Although radio is a good way to reach the young married demographic it does not have the power that television starts to have at this age. What kinds of products do the young married want? What are they willing to buy?

Shopping Dreams

The fact that many young married have a lot of time to shop but not much money leads directly to a certain pattern of shopping for members of this group. In particular it means that this demographic is often shopping for dreams. What this implies is that these shoppers usually cannot afford all of the things they want at once, so instead they spend a lot of time 'shopping' for things that are out of their reach financially. They spend time looking at and browsing for items that they hope to buy in the future, when finances permit.

Shopping for dreams represents a special time in a young married life. It is not often that a couple can share so many dreams and fantasies about the future. It would not even be any fun to suddenly be rich and to be able to afford all of the hoped for items. There is far more pleasure to be gained from the *anticipation* of these purchases and the hopes and dreams that go with it.

The idea of shopping for dreams is a representative indicator of the true spirit of shopping. It shows that often it is not the actual buying of items that is the important part of the process but rather the 'looking forward' to a purchase that gives the shopper enjoyment. For the less well-off young married, this aspect of the shopping experience is dominant and is truly a significant part of the young married life. Almost all older readers will remember a time when they were young and in love and looked forward with great anticipation to the purchase of items that represented the shared dreams of a young life together.

Retailers, manufacturers and advertisers should be able to tap into this dimension of the young married demographic. Eventually this group will buy all of the items they dream about and part of the message to be sent to them should be cognizant of the fact that when it comes to shopping, they are dreamers. Advertisers should be able to appeal to the fact that young marrieds are full of hope and aspirations, and they should strive to satisfy the shopping fantasies that this group exhibits. Retailers should strive to make *their* products the ones that will appeal to the special nature of this group. Products should be targeted to fulfill the dreams of these shoppers.

First-Time Shoppers

First purchases are important. My wife and I still remember clearly the first stereo we bought together at *Radio Shack* for $299. We also remember vividly the first color television that we bought at *Big George's* in Ann Arbor, Michigan for $349. Those very first purchases in the early years of a married life are memorable events. Couples begin sharing a life together and one of the first and most important things they do as a couple is to start making purchases.

Young married shoppers are naïve. They have never bought household furnishings before and so are at the mercy of sales people, retailers and advertisers. What is it that such naïve shoppers are looking for? Although they are shopping on the surface for price and quality there is also a more important dimension to the experience of the first-time shopper. Primarily they are looking to feel good about the purchases they make. They want to feel that they are competent to make such adult decisions in a sensible and mature way. There is a lot to be learned here for retailers. It is essential to make first-time young shoppers feel like they are getting the upper hand in any deal that is made. The twenty-something married shopper wants to feel like he is good at making these adult decisions. First purchases are a defining moment in life and there is nothing more important than coming away from such a purchase feeling confident that a good deal was obtained. In this regard, first-time shoppers can be seen as shopping for self-esteem. It is essential to them to feel good about buying adult products and to feel good about the price and quality obtained.

Having a good experience can keep a first-time shopper a customer for life. A young shopper who feels a sense of self-satisfaction about a major purchase will be comfortable shopping again at the same store. He needs to feel that he was treated with respect, that he got a good deal, and that he made a good decision. Such a customer can also become brand loyal if his first experience is a happy one. All shoppers want to feel that they are good shoppers but this is especially true of the young married group. Their self-esteem is on the line when it comes to making these first-time decisions. More importantly, they also want to impress their friends and relatives with their shopping prowess. While many older shoppers are reluctant to brag about purchases, this is not the case with first-time shoppers, who are anxious to let everyone know about the good deals they got and who are anxious to demonstrate their shopping expertise.

A common mistake that first-time shoppers make with major items is that they do not attempt to negotiate a better price. Usually they are intimidated enough by the whole process of shopping for major items that they loathe asking the salesman for a better deal. Older shoppers become aware that one can almost always do better than the sticker price, but this takes boldness that only comes with experience. Young shoppers should be urged to ask for a better deal whenever they shop – the sales people are almost always accommodating.

Chapter 8

The Busy Demographic:
The Most Important Group

At different stages of life, different things will be important to different shoppers. Each group has its own identity, ideas and desires, and these are unique to each generation. They will reflect not only the wants and needs of a generation but also the 'times' in which it lives. At the same time, the *lifestyle* of any particular group also plays a significant role in shopping behavior. Different groups exhibit different behaviors, depending on their age and demographic membership, and these memberships will influence shopping patterns and behavior. Every age group has shopping preferences that are unique and a part of our interest in looking at shoppers is to look at the unique characteristics of each group.

The busy demographic is the group that is younger than the baby boomers and older than the married twenty-somethings. This demographic group has several interesting features when it comes to shopping. The busy demographic is important. It is the group that is really going to power the malls and the stores in the years to come. But at the same time, this is a group that will be difficult to please when it comes to shopping. This relatively young group is at the busiest time of life when it comes to both work and family life. As a consequence it is a real challenge to meet their shopping requirements. This group is working to establish careers and so is working harder and longer than almost any other. At the same time this group is also trying to raise young families and so time is at a premium. As a result of these twin pressures, retailers will be hard pressed to meet the needs of the busy demographic.

The Most Important Demographic

The busy demographic is the most important one when it comes to shopping. Many writers suggest that it is the baby boomers that are the dominant demographic shopping group. The busy demographic has several factors in its favor as the most important shopping group.

Consider the average member of the busy demographic. They have completed their education. They are married. They have young children, and, they are at the most high-pressure time in their careers. This is the age at which people establish themselves in their jobs. Normally at a very young age workers move from job to job seeking out advancement opportunities and seeking a type of position that is personally rewarding. After a short time they usually settle into a permanent position that offers job security in a time when a young family with children needs it. Typically people work the hardest and longest hours of their lives when they are at this stage of their careers. They are competing with co-workers to advance and to gain job security, and they are beginning to work their way through the hierarchy of positions that exists in almost every place of employment. Family well-being is a high priority. The appearance of young children means a solid paycheck is a necessity and there is little room for 'downtime' career wise. These pressures fall on both male and female members of this group.

When it comes to shopping for the busy demographic there is little room for error. Their busy lives with work and family means time is at a premium and so shopping for this group has to be targeted to save time. Most families with young children live in a *time-pressed* world where there never seem to be enough hours in the day to get things done. Jobs are demanding, extended hours of work are expected, and other daily activities demand attention. Children need to be driven to piano lessons, soccer practice and swimming classes, there is the PTA meeting to attend, and shopping for groceries to be done for that dinner party on the weekend. Never mind that report that needs to be written by Monday. The time-pressed adult has less of one thing available to her (time) and more of another thing available (money). As a result she is looking for timesaving products and services wherever they are available. A good example of this trend is in the growing use of professional housecleaning services of which more and more shoppers, especially women, are taking advantage. Similarly, some clothing stores are now offering personalized shopping services to men and women whereby seasoned sales staff will help customers outfit themselves with entire wardrobes of matching ensembles all at one time. This personalized service saves the shopper the time of traveling around.

There are other areas in which the busy demographic looks for help in getting things done. Specialized services such as lawn care, nannies, house decorating, and custom car cleaning are becoming more popular as overworked adults look for time relief. When it comes to shopping, the busy demographic wants the retailer to understand his needs. Yes, he wants and needs to shop, and yes, sometimes shopping is essential. When a birthday or anniversary comes up, even the busy professional feels compelled to go on a serious shopping expedition. He or she not only wants to accomplish the task in an efficient manner, but the job should not be so efficient as to seem unemotional or uncaring. The retailer needs to provide an adequate choice of high quality merchandise at a good value. The harried shopper appreciates the convenience that this means but also wants to fully experience the pleasure of shopping and gift buying. It just should not take too long.

The busy demographic has both more money for shopping, and less time for it. Retailers that can accomplish objectives that save time, for example, online grocery shopping and delivery, will find that there is a willing audience for their efforts. Today's young professional does not have time to wander the malls or travel downtown on a leisurely shopping expedition. Neither do they have time to stand in line returning a defective product nor do they have the inclination to drive all over town looking for a particular product. Efficiency and convenience are the watchwords for the retailer, whether it comes to changing oil, selling cars, setting up travel plans or buying groceries. Busy people want speed and no hassles; they want shopping to be but a small part of their lives so there is more room for the big things, like that Christmas concert at the elementary school. On a busy person's slate of priorities, shopping is far down on the list.

Busy people still shop price and value. But they want it quickly and efficiently. One of the reasons for the success of stores like *Price-Costco* is that shoppers know they are getting good quality merchandise at a good price. *Price-Costco* makes shopping decisions easier. Many other chains have similar reputations for value and consumers patronize them because they take the guesswork out of shopping.

When busy people shop, they want the experience to be painless. Consider an example. Suppose a consumer is shopping for a new computer and wants a certain set of features at a good price. The successful retailer will offer this consumer a wide range of product lines that have the features that he wants, will offer headache free sales and service, and will have a reputation for quality so that the customer can be assured that he is getting good value for his dollar. Although this seems like a simple formula for success it is really surprising how many retailers fail to achieve these three basic goals. How many times have you been looking for a particular product only to find that the retailer did not have what you wanted, that the sales staff were uninformed, or that you did not really trust in the product or the store? Good retailers see the willing consumer as presenting a potential sales opportunity that is too good to pass up. They go out of their way to make sure that the three requirements above are satisfied. Meanwhile, busy people see the sales transaction as a means to an end, as a solution to just one more of the list of things that needs to be accomplished.

Conflicting Desires

The busy demographic is fraught with difficulties. One central problem is that they have conflicting desires about what they want to buy. A new career and initial success in that career means money is available to start to buy big-ticket items for the first time. But this group is confused. On the one hand they still want the things they longed for as teens. At the same time, however, this group realizes that it is aging and so it wants to buy the things that are appropriate to its rapidly maturing lifestyle. They want a huge, high-end audio system *and* they want baby furniture. They want a sporty car *and* one that will carry groceries. They want to impress their friends with their fashionable furnishings *and* they want the in-laws to be impressed with their sensibility.

In short, the busy demographic is torn between two sources of demand for products and so are sometimes unsure of what to buy. For the retailer or advertiser this presents an opportunity to frame the appropriate demand in the mind of this shopper. First and foremost it is a time for some retailers to impress on the busy demographic that they are a maturing group and so should be buying the products appropriate to their age. The idea is that mini-van is perfect for you. But at the same time, other retailers will want to convey the message that it is acceptable to indulge one's teen fantasies. In other words, it is all right to indulge oneself in that sports car you always wanted. Both marketing strategies are appropriate to this group and which one is followed depends on the product that is being marketed.

Marketing to Couples

Marketing to this group may involve the exploitation of the shared nature of the shopping experience. Advertising could be directed at the concept that shared items and shared purchases are essential parts of a close relationship. Targeting to this group requires that retailers put themselves in the place of the customer and imagine the emotions and feelings of this young shopper. What kind of products should be marketed to *couples*, as opposed to individuals, and what kinds of products are more likely to benefit from this sort of marketing? The answer is that there are many items that may sell better to a couple. In particular, all kinds of home furnishings are items that are shared. Furniture, home decorations, appliances and home accessories are just a few of the items that imply a strong sense of sharing among couples. Retailers and advertisers could profitably target their efforts towards the shared nature of these products. The goal is to market a product in a way that appeals to both individuals but also to the stronger collective spirit of the couple.

The difference between the sexes is an important one and many marketing studies have tried to uncover the differences between men and women. For the most part such studies find that men are prone to excess and to buying on impulse, whereas women are more likely to be conservative shoppers and more patient. A product that sells to both men and women simultaneously should satisfy this dual nature of the relationship between the sexes. A car, for example, should appeal to the masculine characteristics of the male shopper (lots of power, 'cool' looks) but should also appeal to the female side of the couple (child restraints, safety features). The same kind of logic should apply to all products of interest to couples.

Marketing to couples is a tactic that has been seriously overlooked but is one that is likely to pay dividends. The busy demographic does almost all of its serious shopping in couple format. Except for groceries and some hardware it is difficult to imagine this group shopping alone. For the most part they shop as a couple and make shopping decisions as a couple. And even when it comes to groceries it is becoming ever more likely that couples do it together, with more husbands participating in greater numbers than ever before. Couples share mostly everything and there is no reason why shopping should not be one of the most shared experiences of all.

Clothing

The busy young executive wants to dress smartly and wants to have the look of success. There is a price to pay for this however and that is the time one must invest in shopping for the 'right' clothes. Retailers should try to satisfy all of the busy shopper's needs in a one-stop shopping format. Businessmen want to buy a suit, a coordinating tie and shirt all in one place and with a minimum of fuss. Many stores provide such a service. But how many men's stores simultaneously sell the shoes to complete the outfit? Ideas like these are what will set one retailer apart from the others. The same line of thought goes for women's wear. Although you can buy a suit and coordinating blouse under one roof, it is rare for the same business to also sell coordinating shoes and accessories to complete the outfit. Many businesses can save the shopper valuable time by providing coordinating services like these. There is much to be said for providing a total package of dress in a convenient format.

This generation is sometimes torn between items to wear. They do not want to wear 'kids' clothing but at the same time they do not want to look like their parents either. Do they wear *Tommy* jeans or do they wear *Levi* jeans? Sometimes the choice is not clear. This group presents a tough challenge to the retailer because this is not a group that is typically 'targeted' by manufacturers.

The busy demographic grew up with designer labels and brand names and so is prepared to offer its loyalties to those companies that deliver the appropriate names. Is it possible to buy a *Tommy* suit for example or a *Nike* pair of dress shoes? These are the kinds of product expansions that will keep a brand loyal generation buying as it ages. It would seem that there are a number of different areas for expansion of many product lines.

Housing

The busy demographic is *the* demographic when it comes to housing. This is the demographic group that buys a larger house and, because of this, the clout they have in the housing market is huge. Unlike many products that sell all over the country at a national level, housing is usually a product that is provided by local companies. In spite of this fact, it is quite impressive that most homebuilders stay in step with the times and follow remarkably similar paths to innovation.

Houses change style just like clothing, automobiles, and any other items that follow general fashion trends. Homebuilders are constantly updating features of homes to reflect demand for current styles in the market. Particular features will be in vogue for a limited time, only to be replaced by alternative forms when their 'style' has lost its luster. The only thing constant about the business is change, and there is an endless succession of design and style changes as builders try to stay at the forefront of the industry.

What does the busy demographic look for when it buys a new house? One critical factor that the builder cannot build into the house is its location. When it comes to new houses, the busy demographic looks for a homogenous neighborhood where there will be other children of similar ages and it looks for location with respect to facilities, especially schools. Most young parents would prefer to have their young, elementary age children walk to school so this becomes one of the most important locational factors.

What else does the busy demographic look for in a house? Basically they are at a stage of life where the focus is on the family so anything that relates to strong family qualities will appeal to them. Such things might include a family room, a rec room, a 'lunch counter' in the kitchen, a play area, or storage areas for toys. Builders could do so much more to appeal to this demographic just by building in a few extra features. For example, the standard family designed home has three bedrooms and the kid's rooms usually have a single closet. A simple and attractive innovation would be to build in storage spaces for toys in bedrooms. Such an elementary design change would be a big attraction for many parents. Similarly, a play area close to the bedrooms would be a desirable feature for most parents of young children. There are a lot of simple innovations like this that will make new houses more sellable to the busy demographic. This stage of their life is twofold; there is a concern with careers and there is a concern with building a strong home life. Builders and architects would be wise to play to the strong sense of family that permeates this demographic group.

There are other, more standard features that parents of young children will look for. A multi-car garage with lots of storage space for toys, a mudroom, and large closets are a few more of the types of things that are important. How many times have you looked in a garage on a show-home only to see three blank walls and just enough room for two cars? What about some storage space designed exclusively for toys and bicycles? It is easy to add small features to new houses that will set them apart from the competition.

A large proportion of homebuyers in the busy demographic prefer older homes. There is something attractive about an older home in a well-established neighborhood with mature trees. The retail significance of this trend is with respect to home renovations. There is an enormous market for renovating older homes yet there are very few contractors who advertise themselves for this purpose. The busy demographic is very keen to buy older homes and refurbish and restore them, but they need help in doing so. This is likely a trend that will continue to grow as the size of the available older housing continues to grow. Demographic trends suggest that more older home owners will be ready to put their houses on the market as they reach retirement age, and this means a steady supply of older homes will come on the market for the busy demographic. The busy demographic is not content with houses the way they buy them however. For them it is necessary to completely modernize and brighten these homes until they look like new inside. This means new flooring, new wall coverings, new light fixtures, new trim and renovated woodwork. Such restoration work is expensive, yet there is almost no limit to the extent to which the busy demographic will spend money to get their refurbished homes into the shape they want them to be. Contractors, retailers and advertisers should be aware of the huge trend toward home renovation that exists among this group.

For both old and new homeowners there would also seem to be the potential for a big retail market in decorating. Young homeowners are looking for paint, wallpaper, trim, paintings, plants and other such materials in order to decorate their new homes. Coordinating paint, wallpaper and curtains are another area where there will be strong demand. There is room in the market for more retailers to provide such products to the busy demographic. They are very concerned with enhancing their new or refurbished homes with the latest in home fashions and willing to patronize those businesses that make it simple and convenient for them to do so. Time and accommodation are the watchwords for this demographic and, in spite of their focus on careers, their homes are also a big priority in their lives. Home decorating centers should be very successful in light of the growth in the busy demographic in the years to come. There are literally millions of new and renovated homes just waiting to be decorated and at present the market for this endeavor is fragmented.

The homes of the busy demographic also need to be filled with appliances and electronics. Once again this represents a huge source of demand in the market that probably goes unrecognized by a large portion of marketers. With fresh new houses comes fresh new demand for all kinds of home accessories. In addition to basic everyday appliances (e.g., microwaves) the busy demographic also wants all of the good things in life and they want them now. Home theatre systems, surround sound and big-screen televisions are examples of the belongings that this demographic does not have the patience to wait for. Consider a case in point. As Todd Thibodeaux, chief economist for the Consumer Electronics Manufacturers Association indicates:

> Indeed, fully 20 million Americans have purchased big-screen TVs costing $2000 or more. That figure is all the more striking when you contrast it with the sales curve for color TVs three decades ago. In 1961, the average color TV cost about $2000 in today's dollars, and only 300,000 Americans had one.

What better evidence could there be for the argument that there is a new mode of shopping that exists out there. People are indulging themselves far more than they did in the past for luxury products and this lends credence to the idea that shopping in general has moved to a higher plane of needs. For the busy demographic the evidence suggests that they do not have the patience that their parents had when it comes to buying home furnishings. While their parents may have often been content to save their money and bide their time, this demographic will have none of it. They want what they want, and they do not want to wait for it.

How does the young busy demographic pay for all of these things? Buying on credit is becoming more important. There is less willingness to wait for the good things in life and there is more willingness to buy on time to get what you want right now. Consumers are shopping more by going into debt more. This is a stunning revelation because it means that people are so desperate to buy the things they feel they must have, that they will even go into debt to do so. Being able to afford an item is not really a problem any more. *Feed* magazine writer Ana Marie Cox quotes author Juliet Schor:

> The level of income needed to fulfill one's dream, to satisfy aspirations, doubled between 1986 and 1994 and is currently more than twice the national median income. So, strictly speaking, the massive amount of American consumer debt proves Americans can't afford what they buy. But we want it anyway. And, thanks to credit cards, we get it.

Today's consumer spending is different than that of any other period and surely this lends credence to the argument that there is a new kind of shopping. The busy demographic is impatient to get what it wants and so is more willing than its parents to buy on credit. The message here for retailers is a strong one. Demand for products among this demographic group is so strong that literally nothing will stand in their way of getting what they want. If shopping is made easy, attractive and accessible for this group they will buy what they want, whether they can afford it or not.

Toys and Sports

The number one generation for the purchase of toys and youth sports paraphernalia is the busy demographic. This is the group that has young children and so they single-handedly drive the market for these products. It is easy to see why they are called the busy demographic. In addition to establishing careers and building and furnishing homes they are also raising young children.

For the busy demographic shopping for toys follows the same rules as their other shopping, simplicity and convenience are the order of the day. It is difficult for retailers to stay on top of the game. There are literally thousands of children's products on the market now and, in fact, there are many more choices than there used to be. Nevertheless, the successful retailer will stay on top of trends and will endeavor to keep in stock the latest and hottest items. Turnover is huge in this business as trends and 'popular items' come and go with great frequency. It is up to the merchant to roll over his product lines as quickly as fashion changes with the times.

A big boon in the provision of toys and sports equipment to the busy demographic comes in the form of big box stores. Such stores usually provide selection, price and quality under one roof and make life easier for the busy young professional. Big box stores are a growing phenomenon in toys and sports, as in many other areas, and many smaller retailers will have trouble competing with the volume discount buying that the big stores are able to provide.

The Significance of Big Box Stores

What is it about big box stores that make them such a successful phenomenon? Why is it that this new form of acquiring products has taken the shopping world by storm? A part of the answer is to be found in shoppers like those of the busy demographic. They have a lot of things to buy, not a lot of time to do it, and they are searching for good value. Typically the big box store provides the items that the consumer is looking for. For the shopper who is looking for a particular item, they usually provide a greater selection of goods than is available in a smaller store with less inventory. They have a wide range of goods available, with more products to satisfy a wider range of tastes. And they also have a reputation for providing a good price on items with their well-known status as big discount buyers. Thus the big box store makes it easier for the consumer to shop. There is less running around for product selection and there is less need to go around and comparison shop. Big box stores take the geography out of shopping.

Consumers have taken to the big box stores in droves. The ever-increasing slice of market share that they are taking away from smaller operators evidences their success at what they do. Some existing chains are building their new stores in big box format to enable them to compete better with the already established big box chains. A good example is *Wal-Mart* which has opened Supercenters to include a greater diversity of product lines under one roof.

For the busy demographic, with the huge diversity of household products they need to buy, big box stores represent a new form of convenience. The busy shopper saves time and money at the big box store and so is more willing to patronize them. Are consumers looking for the personal treatment they can get from a small, local store? The evidence suggests not. Price and value are clearly still the bottom line when it comes to product selection and the overwhelming success of big box stores bears this out. Those who suggest that small stores with high quality service are the way of the future are heading down the wrong road. The consumer still knows what he wants and there is no doubt that high quality items at a good price are worth the more impersonal atmosphere of the big box store. Consumers shop for value more than anything.

Chapter 9

The Baby Boomers:
Shopping for Emotional Reasons

Just who are the baby boomers? They are the group of people that was born in the years just after World War II. The war had ended, the economy was ready to boom, people's fears about the future had been relieved and good times had arrived. As a consequence the population birth rate literally exploded in the years immediately after the war and a huge group of people was born. This huge group is known as the baby boomers (born in the economic 'boom' after the war) and they are notorious for their demographic influence. The boomers were born in the years between 1946 and 1964 and they represent an unprecedented 'bulge' in the birth rate statistics for the century. Never before had such a large group of people been born in such a short time span. The boomers are important. Because of the size of the group it has an impact on almost everything around it. The boomers are thought to influence the stock market, housing prices, health care and just about anything else that is inclined to change in response to sheer numbers of people. The boomers are now closing in on the range of forty and sixty years of age and they still have an effect on things around them. One place where the boomers have long driven the numbers is with respect to shopping. This huge group of people has had a decided effect on patterns of consumption over the last fifty years and they continue to do so today.

Consider the impact that they have had on housing prices throughout their lifetimes. They started to enter the housing market in the 1960s and continued to do so in the 1970s. As a consequence housing prices were driven to price levels that had never before been witnessed. Boomers that bought a house in the 1960s were able to sell it twenty years later for tens of thousands of dollars more than they paid for it. In fact it was during this period that people started to believe that the only thing they needed for a retirement nest egg was their house. This has changed dramatically today. As the boomers passed through the system their impact was felt for a time, but then subsided once they all had acquired houses. Prices started to level off and the unprecedented increases that had been witnessed in the years proceeding were a thing of the past. It is easy to see where the boomers will have an impact on housing in the future. They are just starting to hit retirement age now and so we can expect that demand for retirement housing – especially condominiums – will soar in the near future. The boomers will all be ready to retire in the next twenty years and so we can expect unforeseen demand for this kind of housing in the years to come.

Not only are the baby boomers a big group when it comes to numbers but they also carry a lot of weight when it comes to income. The boomers, being at an average age of about forty-five to fifty, are making the most money of their lives. They are at the peak of their income earning years and thus they have lots of money with which to shop. What are some of the things with which they are concerned? Where do the boomers make their impact felt?

The answer is that the boomers have a huge effect on shopping and spending simply by virtue of their numbers. A case in point would be the large number of sport utility vehicles (or SUVs) that one finds on the roads. What is the demographic that is old enough to want these vehicles and that can afford to buy them? The response is that it is the baby boomers that drive trends like this. They are at that stage of life where the psychology of owning a sport UV is right for them and they have the disposable income to get what they want. Automakers know who wants these vehicles and they target their advertising to this demographic group. The advertising slogan appeals to the concept of off-road adventure, featuring SUVs driving through rugged terrain and showing their owners engaged in active sports such as kayaking and hiking. This mentality appeals to the forty-something executive who rarely gets away from her desk. She feels like she deserves the outdoor life of adventure if only she had the time. Buying the sport UV is a chance to express her feelings and desires, even though owning the vehicle will be as close as she will ever get to realizing her outdoor dreams.

The baby boomers are sitting in the drivers seat when it comes to mainline shopping trends for big, expensive and luxury items. Their shopping presence and power is unprecedented. They are the largest, wealthiest demographic of them all.

One needs to consider the major kinds of places where the boomers will spend their money. Houses, cars, cottages and high-end vacation trips are just a few of the places where boomers are making their presence felt. The boomers swagger around in the retail market like bulls in a china shop, buying up whatever they want, whenever they want it. They have lots of disposable income and they are at that stage in life where they realize they are not going to live forever. They are willing and anxious to spend their money and to indulge themselves in the best that life has to offer. A new boat? A cruise? A big screen television? A trip to Hawaii? A new video camera? A sport utility vehicle? The boomers will not deprive themselves.

The Shopping Mindset of the Baby Boomers

The shopping mindset of the baby boomer generation is unique. They have several things that set them apart from every other shopping generation. For one thing this is the first generation that was raised on television. As the first boomers were being born in the late 1940s and early 1950s television was also being invented. This generation was literally weaned on television and its effect on this group is one of the biggest social experiments of all time. We still do not know how television affects people but the boomers were exposed to it from birth without us having any idea of how this new medium would shape their lives.

One thing that many people agree upon is that television alters the attention span. It is a commonly held belief that the quick clips, and flips, of television have an effect on how we perceive the world. For the boomers, raised on television for the first time, one wonders how the impact of television affects shopping behavior. When it comes to shopping do the boomers have short attention spans, do they have a tendency to switch or flip quickly from item to item? Do they require instant gratification, where the rewards of an action are received immediately following behavior? The suspicion is that, yes, these are behaviors that are characteristic of boomer shopping. One suspects that when they shop in stores, boomers do not have the patience of their parents. One suspects that they are in a hurry, are impatient and are difficult to please. It may be that it requires a more intensive effort on the part of retailers and advertisers to catch the attention of the *television-brained* baby boomer. In addition it would appear that boomers are pleased with the instant gratification of shopping. For most shopping behavior the rewards are immediate and this is the lifestyle with which boomers have grown up.

A second way in which television affects the boomers is that they are a generation that has grown up seeing more advertisements than any other generation in history. When the five-year old boomer started watching television in the 1950s she also started watching ads. *Captain Kangaroo* came with advertisements, as did every other new show at the time. This is truly the first generation that has been raised on a steady and daily diet of television advertising. How does this history affect the shopping and retail behavior of the boomers? How does a generation shop that has been inundated with ads since birth? How does this generation pay attention to advertising today, given the way they have been raised? Undoubtedly the boomers are indifferent to much modern advertising. Anyone who has grown up with as much advertising as the boomers would have to be insulated to its effects. One expects that boomers have been so saturated with ordinary, everyday advertising that it is only exceptional ads that catch their attention. One would need only to survey a television watcher at the end of an evening's diet of television ads to find which if any of them are remembered.

It may only be repetition that works with the boomers. Maybe they have to see that ad for *Coca-Cola* innumerable times for it to have an impact on their buying decision. There are a lot of mysteries in advertising and a lot of unknowns but one thing we can say for sure is that the baby boomers have been so overwhelmed by ads in their lives that they must be largely indifferent to them unless they are exceptional. Readers may remember an ad that asked, "How does the guy who drives the snow plough get to work?". The answer was that he drove a *Volkswagen Beetle*. That ad has been judged to be one of the best of all time and it is a certainty that people who saw the ad remember it. It is just one example of the kind of ad that may be required to grab the boomers attention. Any ad competes with all of the other ads for the mindset of the shopper and it is only those that stand above the crowd that will come out as winners.

A third way that the baby boomers may have a unique mindset for shopping is that they are the most overindulged generation in the history of shopping. The boomer grew up in the post-war times when the economy was booming and they were indulged by their parents at ever opportunity. They had more things bought for them than any generation that went before, from when they were young children right up to today. The boomers have never been denied anything and so as they reach adulthood and shop for themselves they still are not to be denied. What this generation wants it gets. It always has and it always will. How does this affect the shopping behavior of the boomers? One thing it means is that if advertisers and producers can invent demand for new products the boomers will line up to buy it. A case in point is the SUV that was 'invented' just a few years ago. Meanwhile the manufacturers cannot make the product fast enough to satisfy the boomers who buy it. Virtually every leading manufacturer has launched a line of SUVs in order to cash in on the action. These vehicles are expensive, yet the boomers who want them, buy them, even if they have to do it on credit. This generation is not to be denied the things that it wants.

Boomers shop the levels. In particular, they shop the fifth level. Since they have acquired most of life's basic necessities, they shop the highest levels of the shopping pyramid most often. They are often shopping for the self, to define the self, and for self-fulfillment. In short they are shopping to self-actualize. In many cases, they have achieved their need to belong and they have achieved self-esteem. When it comes to shopping they set their sights higher – they shop for the soul, for the inner self and for the pleasures of shopping itself. Boomers are often on a higher plane when it comes to shopping and manufacturers, retailers and advertisers should be acutely aware of this phenomenon. This group is hard to please and products must be targeted at just the right level in order to catch the fancy of this group. Boomers are ready to achieve personal growth and a sense of accomplishment through their shopping.

The 'Forever Young' Theory of Marketing

One of the most intriguing theories that can be put forward about the baby boomers is to say that they never really grew up. Thus products that are targeted at younger shoppers will also appeal to the boomers. There is an idea to back up this theory. There is an old saying in the automobile sales business that says, "You can sell a young man's car to an old man, but you cannot sell an old man's car to a young man". There is an air of truth in this idea and there is no reason why it cannot be applied to other products. It says more generally that you can sell 'young' products to older people, but you cannot sell 'old' products to young people. This suggests that people, as shoppers, never really grow out of their youthful years. The same style of car that appealed to someone when they were twenty will also appeal to them when they are fifty. Similarly, the same style of clothing that attracted someone in their teens will be attractive to them when they are in their forties. This 'Forever Young' Theory applies widely to any number of products and to virtually any age group. It especially applies to the boomers as they try to recreate their youth through their shopping behavior. Products that appealed to the boomer in his teens and twenties will also appeal to him in his forties and fifties. For the retailer and especially the advertiser the message is clear. It is necessary to try to appeal to the boomer as if he is still in his youth. This seems to be a reliable way to target advertising and retail sales to this demographic group.

The 'Forever Young' Theory of shopping has profound implications for demographic targeting. It says that shoppers are 'forever young' and suggests therefore that targeting should be directed primarily at young shoppers. This offers a sound explanation for the way that the market has evolved to the present point. We know that most advertising and marketing is directed to younger segments of the market and this theory explains why. But it also indicates that if marketers are explicitly targeting older demographic groups that they should set their sites on advertising to younger groups. There are *real targets* in marketing but that there are also *virtual targets*. It says that if you want to sell clothing to a baby boomer (the real target) that your advertising should focus on younger age groups (the virtual target). It says that if you want to sell a sport UV to a fifty-year old, real target, you should direct your ad to a twenty-year old, virtual target. This theory of marketing applies to all older shoppers at almost all times. It says they think of themselves as being younger than they are and, when it comes to advertising, they want to be treated as being younger.

The 'Forever Young' Theory applies to all manner of products. Imagine that we want to sell *Pepsi* to baby boomers. The theory says that they will not be turned on by ads that depict fellow baby boomers consuming *Pepsi*. Instead it says that they want to see youthful people – their image of themselves – consuming the product. Imagine similarly that you are designing condominiums for retiring baby boomers. There might be a tendency by some designers to incorporate older features with which the baby boomers are familiar. The theory says the condos should be designed with all of the latest features that appeal to youth. Apply this theory to just about all products for the boomers and you have the secret to success for selling to this age segment of the population.

Vehicles

What is it that drives the baby boomers when it comes to automobiles? An interesting story comes from the minivan, which is a great example of a baby boomer success story. When *Chrysler* invented the minivan in the 1980s the company was in totally unexplored territory. They took a big chance on a radical new design for a vehicle. Coincidentally the baby boomers were entering their childbearing years at the same time and so were looking for a vehicle that would be appropriate to family use. The fit between the new vehicle and the demographics of the day was a perfect one and *Chrysler* had a runaway hit on their hands. This is a good illustration again of the marketing potential of the baby boomers. They have an important influence on demand.

What are the other types of vehicles that baby boomers want? This is a big group – it spans twenty years – and so it is hard to say that the demographic is entirely consistent in what it wants. It would seem convenient however to divide the boomers into two big groups when it comes to vehicles. On the one hand there are the older baby boomers who are content to drive a traditional sedan. There are still a lot of these on the roads and behind the wheel of most of them you will find a baby boomer. On the other hand there are those baby boomers – presumably the younger ones – that are more interested in a youthful or upscale vehicle. Thus we not only see the trend towards sport utility vehicles but also towards sports cars and especially upscale models such as the *Acura* or *Lexus*. In the latter case we have well-off boomers who are anxious to spend their money on the finer things in life. They are seeking rewards for their life's work and are keen to compensate themselves for their accomplishments.

An excellent example of the impact of the boomers is found in the recent decision of *General Motors* to discontinue the *Oldsmobile* division of the company in its entirety. *General Motors* exhausted itself trying to revive the *Oldsmobile* line. Older models such as the *Delta 88* and *Cutlass* were replaced with newer ones, but to no avail. *GM* hoped to appeal to middle-aged drivers with the new models but they did not catch on. What is the reason for this? Probably a central issue is that to baby boomers the *Oldsmobile* is the car that your Dad drove. The boomers want to be different. Thus the boomers, with their very specialized demand, have managed to close down an entire division of the biggest car company in the world. The *Oldsmobile* line hit its zenith in the 1950s and 1960s when the parents of the baby boomers were buying new cars every few years. In recent times the boomers, and the busy demographic, have shunned the brand and thereby drove it into decline. Product demand, or a lack of it, among the boomers can have significant consequences.

When it comes to shopping for vehicles the boomers often indulge their teenage fantasies for sporty cars. One need only note the redesign of cars that has occurred over the last few years to appreciate that the market is being driven, in part, by baby boomers. Almost all old-style sedans have been replaced with sportier looking models as automobile manufacturers try to target an aging audience. The *Oldsmobile Cutlass*, the car that belonged to the boomer's Dad, has been discontinued and replaced by new models that are shaped like they are made for racing. Boomers are buying the cars they longed for when they were younger and now they can afford to indulge themselves. For automobile retailers, the boomers represent a group that is economically successful and ready to indulge its most expensive fantasies. Men and women alike buy cars that make them feel good and practical considerations take a back seat to the emotional uplift that the vehicle provides. The boomer that has worked hard to get where she is wants to indulge herself when she drives home from work. The feeling is that the vehicle provides a reward for the day's effort.

There is room to expand in the design of vehicles. In particular it would seem that this is an area where the use of designer labels could be applied. Most people will be familiar, for example, with the '*Eddie Bauer*' version of a popular minivan that is available. It is quite surprising that automobile manufacturers have not extended this line of thinking to other well-known names. It is certainly possible to envisage, for example, a car or sport utility vehicle with a brand name label on it in recognition of a set of options where interior design is given an emphasis. Many other such marketing strategies are possible when it comes to co-branding vehicles in this manner. This is a natural way to design vehicles for younger generations that have grown up with designer labels as a central part of their lives. *Ford* or *GM*, for example, could embellish their branding by co-branding with other popular designer label names. A car with an interior by *DKNY*; a sport UV with an interior by *Calvin Klein*? Why not? This is an area of marketing that is ripe for exploitation.

Boomers shop for emotional reasons and so when they buy a product they are expecting a psychological lift. A vehicle that has lots of options or a large engine will not be popular unless it also contains elements that provide for the soul of the shopper. This is the big attraction of SUVs. It is not the vehicle itself that is popular – after all it is really just a pick-up truck with a back on it – but rather it is the emotional content of the vehicle that sells. Surveys show that people who buy SUVs do so for the 'feel' of the vehicle and the rugged, off-road image it presents. It is all about the emotions that the vehicle provides for the owner and it is this that car manufacturers have to come to appreciate to a greater degree. Whether it is a sport UV, a luxury sedan, or a sporty looking sedan, it is the psychological substance of the vehicle that sells.

Housing

When it comes to homes and furnishings the boomer group is definitely upscale. A big house in the suburbs, tastefully furnished, is what is wanted. Making a good appearance when entertaining friends and neighbors is important. The presence of the baby boomers in the housing market has steadily driven up housing prices since the early 1970s. The boomers born in the years after 1945 were ready to buy houses by the time they were in their mid twenties, that is, by about 1970. Similarly, the boomers born by 1965 were ready to buy houses by about 1990. Their huge demand for housing drove the market for over twenty years. And, even though the last of the boomers have bought their houses, demand continues unabated, as the *children* of the boomers continue the market pressure. Boomers born in the 1950s, for example, now have children in their mid-twenties and they too are ready to buy houses. The upward pressure on prices is likely to continue as the children of the boomers continue to grow into the age of buying their first house.

Buying housing is shopping for the psyche. Although there are certain practical features of a house that are of interest to buyers, such as the number of bedrooms or baths, the fact of the matter is that buying a house is very much an exercise in shopping for the mind. A house has to have a certain style, ambiance, or 'air' about it to appeal to buyers. It is a very personal process and there is almost no telling what will or will not interest any given buyer. Real estate agents will attest to the capricious nature of homebuyers and the extent to which the process is a psychologically deep and personal one. In spite of these mental aspects of the home buying process however there are undoubtedly certain features that appeal to the baby boomers. Street appeal is an important feature although this is often in the eye of the beholder. The neighborhood is important, as is the view. In addition, the salient features of the house, such as the entry, the kitchen, the master bedroom and so on, must have a certain level of visual appeal to the buyer. For the boomers the market has been filled with houses with all of this and more. Curved staircases, walk-in pantries, gas fireplaces, hardwood flooring, European kitchens, vaulted ceilings and many more such features that make a house a 'showcase' have been important to the boomers. Their houses are a statement of themselves – of their success in work and in life. It is the boomer's way of exhibiting his or her lifestyle and financial means. A house says a lot about its owners and, with the boomers, houses have become more of an expression of personal psychology than they ever have before.

The baby boomers are the first generation to be able to afford big houses on a grand scale. While the parents of many of the boomers tend to own small-scale bungalows, their offspring demand big houses. In the jargon of the real estate business, the idea was to "buy all the house you can afford". In other words, buy the biggest house you can manage to pay for. That is just what the boomers did and they were able to buy big. There is now a glut of 2400+ square foot houses on the market that are less popular with up and coming generations. Boomers had a profound impact not only on the number of house sales but also on the style and size of houses that were being built. Some forecasters are saying that there are so many large boomer houses on the market – or soon will be – that many of them are going to end up being converted into multiple bedroom care homes for the elderly. The argument is that there just is not enough demand in the housing market for so many large homes.

The future of housing for boomers is in condominiums. They will be able to sell their big houses at big prices and will be looking for housing to take them into their retirement years. Right now many of the boomers are waiting for the children to leave home – the kids are in their early twenties and just finishing up their college education – and once they do, those big houses will go on the market. But just like everything else they do, the boomers will impact the housing market for condos. Not only can we expect pricing pressure in this segment of the market but the boomers will also be particular in what they want. Remember this is the most overindulged generation in history. They will want upscale condos not only with all of the features you would expect but also with those you do not. Gated communities, community pools, a place with a view, a gourmet kitchen and so on are just some of the kinds of things that the boomers will demand. They will not only have the cash but they are of the mindset that whatever they buy must be special; it must be satisfying to the psyche and uplifting to the soul. The ideal condo for the baby boomer will appeal to their psychological profile as being part of the generation that always expects *more*. And gets it.

Clothing

When it comes to clothing, many of the boomers struggle to stay in style. As middle-aged professionals most of them will be sharply dressed. They will look for value and especially convenience when it comes to buying clothes. They will wear the uniform of their generation and, when it comes to work and leisure, they will be concerned with keeping up with their peer group. Some of them try to emulate teenagers in their manner of dress, in a futile attempt to hold onto their youth. It is not uncommon to see adults trying to wear the same designer labels as the teens. Grown-up men and women will wear *Tommy Hilfiger* and *Calvin Klein* in an attempt to show that they are in step with the times. Such efforts are largely in vain. The teens are always several steps ahead and to them, such adults usually look foolish. Better to let the adults wear their old-fashioned *Levi* jeans and to let them feel at one with their own peer group than to try to look like teenagers. There are too many brands and the ones that are in style at any given moment change so quickly that only teens can keep up with the flux. Who else has time for this? *Nautica*? *Max Azria*? *Tommy Hilfiger*? *John Varvatos*? *DKNY*? Only the teens are in tune with the fashion labels because *they* themselves determine what is 'cool'. Keeping up with the latest trends is almost impossible for the average, busy adult.

What is the baby boomer to do when it comes to dress? Should he or she even wear jeans? Are they right for this group or are they too juvenile for such a demographic? The baby boomers are in an extremely difficult position when it comes to shopping for clothing. They have enough disposable income to buy whatever they want but are often at a loss as to what to purchase. In a youth driven market, it is nearly impossible for the middle-aged baby boomer to shop for clothing. Half of it seems too young and the other half seems too old.

Clothing retailers would be wise to try to make the baby boom shopper feel comfortable with herself and her age group. Is it possible to find clothes that are in style but that are not teen copycats? This is the secret to dressing the boomers. They want to feel comfortable and in style, but they do not want to try to look like they are sixteen-years old either. It is a difficult challenge, and retailers and manufacturers do indeed struggle to try to find the pulse of the baby boom generation when it comes to clothing. The most appropriate casual clothing seems to be those that have a certain sense of youthfulness but at the same time send a message that they are definitely for adults. Designer labels are all right, but they need to be small and subtle. For the boomers, clothing has to strike a chord between being grown-up but also not being old. In the same way that teens do not want to dress like their parents, the baby boomers do not want to dress like their own mothers and fathers either. They had their own look when they were teens and they still want to maintain that sense of identity. As a result, this is one of the most difficult markets for clothing retailers to target.

Providing clothing for the boomer demographic presents a tall order for marketers. The baby boom generation is also busy. They have careers, they have families, and they have lots of activities to keep them running. They do not have a lot of time to spend shopping for clothes. Successful retailers will provide one-stop shopping to the bustling boomer. Whether they are shopping for casual wear or for work-wear, they will want a maximum of convenience and minimum of fuss. At the same time it is very important to realize that price levels are probably not a very big obstacle for the busy baby boomer. Their egos are such that they are very serious about looking good, and they are undoubtedly willing to pay a higher price if a retailer has the appropriate clothing to satisfy their difficult tastes. A good example of this margin of price that the boomer is willing to pay is found in upscale designer label clothes for adults, such as the *Ralph Lauren* brand, which charges a premium price for its line of clothes. There is a huge untapped market out there for other retailers, especially those with designer labels, to create fashion trends for the baby boom generation and to satisfy this *clothing-challenged*, wealthy generation.

The Golden Years of Shopping

An interesting question to ask is to consider what type of shoppers the baby boomers are. In the first instance we can say that the boomers have plenty of disposable income. The youngest boomers will be forty in 2005 and so they are still at the stage where they are time-pressed in their daily activities. For these shoppers time is at a premium and they are concerned with getting the maximum amount of shopping done in the minimum amount of time. The oldest boomers will be sixty in 2005 and for these shoppers time is less important. Their children have left home and so they have the leisure hours to spend on more, not less, shopping.

For the forty-something boomer, the children are still at home and so the days and hours are filled largely with children's activities. Soccer, hockey, baseball, swimming, figure skating, dancing, and all of the other daily activities of young adolescent children. For these boomers their lives are still child-centered and so time for shopping is hard to find. At the same time, career pressures continue to be an important factor. These boomers are at the stage where, more than anything, shopping must be fast and convenient. These are not shoppers who want to spend a whole afternoon looking around for a good price on a sound system. They want to shop at a store that offers a good choice of product and one that usually guarantees a low price. For this shopper, big box stores are the answer. They usually offer excellent product selection at discount prices and, while they do make the shopping experience impersonal, they also provide good value together with convenience. This shopper is not interested in comparing the fine points of the products at which he is looking. He just wants to get a good product at a good price, and he wants to do it with a minimum of fuss.

For the sixty-something boomer, the children have left the nest and there are many hours of leisure time to be filled. For this shopper, the shopping experience itself becomes a form of recreation that fills the empty hours now that there are no children's activities to keep him busy. For this baby boomer, shopping becomes an end in itself, an activity that is enjoyable and done with pleasure. This is quite a shift from the forty-something baby boomer. Shopping as a necessary annoyance, to shopping as a form of leisure activity, is one that marks the maturation of the baby boomer. As children's activities and career pressures wind down for the aging baby boomer, the whole nature of shopping as a leisure activity changes. For the sixty-something boomer it is acceptable to spend serious time comparing the virtues of a product. In fact it becomes an enjoyable experience. For this baby boomer, it would not be unusual to spend many days over the course of weeks or months comparison shopping. This is not to say that this shopper will not end up buying the product at the same big box retailer anyway, only that he will spend much more time shopping for it.

There is a serious change that overtakes the life of the baby boomers. They live through the shift from full nest to empty nest, and so their lives undergo a formidable transformation between forty and sixty. The very nature of shopping converts for them from an activity that is just a bother, to one that is pleasant. Retailers and advertisers need to be aware that when the boomer undergoes this mid-life transition his whole life changes. Not only is shopping a more enjoyable experience but this boomer is now shopping for and buying many of the things that he just did not have time for in the past. Thus there is a resurgence of shopping interest among fifty-something baby boomers as they enter *the golden years of shopping* and retailers should be prepared to cater to this important new source of demand.

For the fifty to sixty-something baby boomer, quality of service becomes a much more important consideration. This is a shopper that is taking his time and so wants the full attention of a knowledgeable staff. He is doing serious comparison shopping and is looking not just for a quick purchase of a marginally acceptable product. Rather he is looking at the details of the products he is shopping for. This is a shopper that has all the time in the world and so he is a fussy customer. Sales staff must be prepared to offer whatever it takes to please this shopper. The golden years of shopping are crucial for retailers if they can provide *quality and service* to the rejuvenated baby boomer. Retailers that can deliver this high quality service will be the ones that will be successful with the older baby boomer.

The baby boomers are also the prime age group to be concerned with luxuries such as cottages and family trips to one-stop destinations. This group has made it financially and so all of the upscale extras are part of the package.

Inheritances

No discussion of the boomer generation should take place without mentioning that this group also stands to inherit huge sums of money. Many of them have already discovered this sudden source of income while many more are at the threshold of instant wealth. The boomers are now closing in on the age range between forty and sixty which suggests that their parents are between the ages of approximately sixty-five and eighty-five. There is a huge bubble of saved wealth that is about to come into the hands of the baby boomers as their parents pass away. This group, that is already in a high-income bracket, stands to have even more spending power in the years to come.

One place where the current and future wealth of the baby boomers is of huge interest is in the field of finance and investment. Most financial advisors are really in the business of selling investment vehicles such as mutual funds, and so there is a major area of growth in the future of the financial services retail sector. Cash rich baby boomers will be looking for places to invest their newly acquired inherited wealth. Wise sellers of these products will be prepared to fill this demand. While the boomers are anxious to spend lots of their cash and get all the good things in life, they are also at the age where they are starting to worry about retirement. For them, this means making proper investments for the future so that their affluent lifestyle can continue into their retirement years.

Reinventing Demand

Baby boom generations flush with inherited cash means a continuing high demand for all of the expensive items that people used to just dream about. The boomers are the wealthiest generation of all time and their shopping needs and desires are unprecedented. If you think they have spent a lot so far, just wait until they inherit their parents' estates. Retailers would be smart to create new areas of demand for the boomers. Many of the members of this generation are literally saturated with all of the goods and services they could possibly want. They have been able to shop for, and acquire, almost every possible thing they can imagine, from the big house and the big trips to the luxury cars and the expensive clothing. They have everything they ever hoped for and indeed the marketers have run out of ideas for products they can sell the baby boomers. What do you buy for someone who has everything they could possibly want? It is up to the manufacturers, the retailers and the advertisers to answer that question. There is no doubt that there is pent-up demand out there for shopping of all kinds.

Alternatively, there is room to *reinvent demand,* to recreate demand in traditional areas where it has lagged behind. An excellent example of this is found in the revival of bookstores, which has taken place through the emergence of the giant big box, superstore bookstores. Although this trend may seem just to have reinvigorated interest in books, the more likely truth is that this phenomenon has simply tapped into the baby boom market at the right time. As the boomers age, they settle into more sedate leisure time activities such as reading. The big box bookstores have taken advantage of this resurgence of demand for books among baby boomers and reinvented demand where it had not previously been. There is a lesson to be learned in this. There is room to recreate demand in other areas of interest to aging boomers. Examples that come to mind include such sedentary activities as gardening, traveling, taking cruises, watching television, sewing, cooking and so on. There is likely to be growth in demand for any area that will keep the boomers occupied as they enter their years of greater leisure time.

Boomers shop just like teens. They not only shop to reward themselves, they also shop to emulate their peers. This is a very important time in life, for it is the time when people really start to measure their success in life by the things they own, and by the experiences they purchase.

Middle-aged happiness involves 'keeping up with the Joneses'. The baby boomers aspire to have all of the fine things in life, and at this stage people seem convinced that happiness can only be obtained through purchases. Thus one gauges one's place in the world through the products that one has accumulated, and further satisfaction is acquired largely by additional shopping. The manufacturers and retailers do an admirable job of creating new demand by inventing new products and services that middle-aged consumers will be sure to want. The home theatre system represents an excellent example of such a new, highly demanded product that did not even exist ten years ago. Those in the business of selling continue to invent new products and experiences for the well-off, middle-aged shopper that conveys a sense of personal well-being, extravagance and especially, success. The middle-aged shopper rewards himself for the prosperity he has achieved in life and career through his purchases. By buying a large new boat, or taking the family on a cruise, he pays himself for the success he has achieved. Retailers and salespeople want to keep in mind that the middle-aged shopper is not buying just merchandise – he is celebrating his achievements in life – and should be treated accordingly.

While baby boom shoppers might pride themselves on being mature shoppers that can spot a bargain, the truth of the matter is that when it comes to self-reward, the actual dollar costs of purchases may not be that significant. In the same way that the pre-teen or the teenager will pay exorbitant costs for the correct fashions and labels, adults too will often pay whatever it takes to achieve success in rewarding themselves, and in making a statement. The high-end sport UV, for example, totally unnecessary for driving in the city, represents an excellent instance of the kind of situation in which adults will pay a heavy price to 'keep up with the Joneses' and to stay in style. In this context, adults are just as guilty as teens of following the crowd, and buying things just for appearances. In fact, the adults are worse than the teens, because the sums they spend to impress their peers can be much greater than those that a teen will spend. And the sport UV is just one example. Big-ticket items such as a new house, a new boat, or a new motor home are other examples of how middle-aged people indulge themselves while simultaneously keeping up with their peers. But the sport UV is an excellent example for retailers because, just like the home theatre system, it illustrates a situation where a high level of new demand was created for a new product that did not previously exist. This is marketing at its optimum; creating fresh demand for a fresh product.

Upgrading

Boomers are upgraders. Even though they have most of the things they need in life, when it comes to shopping, they have a tendency to want to upgrade their possessions. This presents a huge opportunity for the retail market. Old stereo systems are replaced by new sound systems, old furniture is upgraded to leather, a regular television set is replaced by one with a giant screen, kitchens are remodeled, appliances are replaced, and so on. There is always something better, newer, or bigger to buy. Upgraders like to be given the opportunity to upgrade. Taking that old television to the cottage, or giving it away to the children that are setting up a household, provides the perfect excuse to upgrade.

Food

When it comes to food, the baby boom demographic presents a stark contrast to the teen and young adult market. While middle-agers occasionally indulge themselves in fast food, by and large this is the demographic that supports the mainstream, sit-down restaurant business. As a consequence, this group sets the standard for high quality restaurant fare and expects a lot for its money. There are fads in restaurants, just like in other things, but eventually quality wins out. The importance of the restaurant market is growing. More people are eating out more often. Many restaurants have had to adjust as people's tastes have matured and expanded through time. Restaurant themes and menus have gotten more exotic as the growing wealth of the baby boom generation has enabled it to indulge itself of better restaurants more often. Quality food and good service are the order of the day, and most people are willing to pay a premium price to get what they want. Retailers would be wise to realize that the middle-aged diner does not just want to buy a meal – rather she is buying an 'experience'.

The Aging Baby Boomer

Boomers born in 1946 will be fifty-five in 2006, and so will start to look forward to retirement. The major event that will happen in the lives of most of the boomers is that their children will grow up and leave the nest. This will have a profound effect not only on their daily lives but also on their spending and shopping habits. The aging boomers will no longer be shopping for a household full of people; instead they will be buying for a two-person household and this will have a major impact on the retail sector. Those boomers that could always be counted on to buy the latest product, whether a sport UV or a home theatre system, will no longer be as important to the market as they once were. How will these aging boomers have an impact on retail systems? What will be their effect on the economy?

One area where the aging boomers will have a huge impact in the years to come will be in the areas of financial planning and advice. We have already discussed the fact that the large group of boomers stands to inherit huge sums of money as their parents pass away. We have a whole generation here that is about to come into significant wealth through inheritances. Boomers will be looking for investment advice and the whole group of them is standing at the threshold of needing financial assistance. One area where this will have a considerable impact is with respect to areas of investment. While many baby boomer investors will look directly to the stock market as a place to invest, the majority of them will probably seek a safer haven for their money in the form of mutual funds. Growth in the mutual fund industry has been incredible over the past ten years and all indications are that this growth will continue in the future as the baby boomers look for a place to invest their new found wealth. At the same time, as the baby boomers age, they get closer to retirement, and so saving for the future becomes a much bigger priority in their lives.

Along with financial planning comes thoughts of early retirement. The aging baby boomers are a prime group for early retirement for several reasons. First, they are a generation that has always been different than their forebears. While the boomer's parents may have worked diligently until sixty-five, the boomer himself wants something unlike his parents had. Second, the boomers as a group will have likely achieved most of their career goals and aspirations by the time they hit their fifties and so they will be looking for other challenges in life. Third, the boomers march to the beat of a different drummer and always have. They are looking for something different in life – something beyond the everyday humdrum existence of work. And they will be determined to find it. Finally, the boomers as a group are the first demographic to have the wealth to be able to retire early. For their parents, it was not an option, but for them, it is.

Next to the kids leaving home, the early retirement of the aging boomers will be the biggest event to happen to this generation. Not only will they be empty-nesters, but they will be finished with work and they will have unprecedented wealth. Just imagine the very thought of millions of boomers, retired from work, cash in hand, and looking for something to do. There is a huge retail and marketing future yet to be realized in the life spans of the boomers. Even as they hit their golden years their impact on markets has not diminished.

One area where aging boomers are expected to have a big financial impact in the coming years is with respect to second houses or vacation properties. With their inherited wealth the older boomers will be looking toward investing in a cottage, retirement home, or 'second' home as a place to get away from it all. To this point in their careers this may be one of the big-ticket items that has eluded them but with new money coming in, owning a second residence becomes a reality. Especially popular in this regard will be cottages that are within commuting distance of large cities. In addition, resort homes in warm destinations will become important for northern residents, as will a place in the mountains for those living in more hospitable climates. Prices for resort and cottage properties are already on the rise and this trend can only continue as the aging boomers look for more things to do with their lives once the children are gone.

Cruises and expeditions should turn out to be another source of great interest to the leisurely late baby boomers. With time and money on their hands they will be looking to do things that are restful, relaxing and laid back. Ocean cruises fit nicely in this regard as do expeditions to exotic locations. Demand for cruises is growing greatly and spectacular new cruise ships are being built all the time. A good example of this trend is found in the construction of the Queen Mary II, which will be the largest ocean liner in the world, stretching longer than three football fields. Analyst Scott Barry of Credit Suisse First Boston writes:

> It is aimed at aging baby boomers who can afford the luxury and time for leisurely transatlantic cruising. The demographics point to an opportunity there. I think the Queen Mary name still has sizable brand equity. It harkens back to the day of white-glove, luxury, old-style cruising. There's a significant nostalgia appeal in the baby boomers. These retirees have the time and the money.

Boomers will have a big influence in another area. Gambling is a source of leisure activity for a growing segment of society and the aging boomers, with their available cash and free time, are a likely source of gambling revenue in the foreseeable future. Statistics show that more money is now being spent in casinos than on any other form of gambling. Literally billions of dollars are spent at gambling, whether it is on lottery tickets, horse races, video terminals or on casinos. Studies show that gambling is most popular among people between the ages of forty-five and sixty-four, that is, the boomers. The number of casinos is growing and now more than ever attending a casino is seen as a natural part of virtually every vacation trip. Gambling has become more socially acceptable, as the boomers have pushed demand in this area, and this shows once again how this generation has a major effect on the markets around it.

As the baby boomers approach mid-life they will have fewer responsibilities at work. Climbing the career ladder will become less significant to them as they see the years slipping by. This lifestyle trend will further enhance their shopping interest in activities that fill leisure time. Of course, when *they* begin these pastimes they suddenly take on greater significance than ever before. This is, after all, the self-centered generation. Nevertheless there should be reinvigorated demand in all sedate areas of leisure activities, especially those that are home-based such as hobbies and crafts. The Internet also comes to mind as a place for shopping and other activities that can take place in the home. Any activities that fill leisure time will take on much greater retail significance.

As the baby boomers age, they will suffer the empty nest syndrome. Children will grow up and leave, and boomers will be left behind. All of those activities and errands that used to be associated with the children's lives will cease to exist and this means that still more leisure time will become available to aging boomers. One might expect that with more leisure time, boomers would spend more time shopping. The problem is that they have fewer things to buy. With the children gone, expenditures on furnishings, toys, household repairs, hardware and, a lot of recreational equipment go by the wayside. While these elderly boomers will have more time and more money than ever before, they have fewer things to buy than ever before. It is up to the merchandisers to invent and reinvent demand. If there is anything that will sell to older shoppers it is nostalgia and a lot of retailers are tapping into this vein of demand by offering old songs, old movies, old television and even housewares and furnishings. *Restoration Hardware*, a chain that specializes in selling home furnishings that have an antique look, is a good example of this nostalgia trend in action.

One area where aging boomers will be very interested in shopping is when it comes to buying things for grandchildren. It is surprising that there is not yet a chain store, such as *Grandparents R Us* or *Grandma's* stores to cater to this demographic that will grow in importance. Grandparents need guidance when it comes to buying toys, games, and especially clothing for their grandchildren and a store that would provide this guidance would probably find itself a success. Undoubtedly, well-off grandparents would be willing to pay a premium price for merchandise that will bring smiles to their grandchildren.

A growing concern for retailers with respect to the aging baby boomers should simply reflect the fact that as people get older they get more budget-minded. As prices of goods and services continue to escalate, many older shoppers lose touch with price trends and are shocked when they finally do discover newly inflated prices. Sticker shock is the well-known phrase that describes this phenomenon and it comes from the auto-retailing world. It refers to the fact that people are sometimes shocked by the list price of new vehicles. This is all the more true if people have not bought a new car in quite a while and so are unused to the new vehicle prices. For the aging baby boomer, sticker shock becomes an almost daily occurrence as prices of all items rise steadily. Money becomes dearer as people age and older shoppers are more reluctant to part with a dollar. For all their bravado, this facet of life will start to slowly creep into the baby boomers lives over the coming years. For the retailer this is disappointing news. It says, as the boomers get older that they will become more reluctant shoppers, less willing to purchase goods that they see as having prices too high.

As people age, they buy things less often. A pair of shoes that used to be worn for a year suddenly lasts much longer. A coat that used to go out of style after a year or two now seems to last for many years. Shirts, pants, tops, and sweaters that previously were put in storage after a year or so of use now continue to be used for several years. In the world of the older person, time passes by faster and faster. As it does, shopping takes place less and less. "I thought I just bought that last year" might be the phrase used to describe a dress that is three years old. "That's nearly brand new" might be used to depict a suit that is five years old. As time passes by more quickly, purchased items have their shelf life extended. This means that as people get older they shop less often and this will occur for the aged baby boomers just like it does for everyone else. There is little retailers can do about this phenomenon save for being aware of it and trying to encourage older shoppers to be more amenable to replacing items like they did when they were younger.

As an ever-widening segment of the shopping community gets older, product mix and selection will reflect these demographic changes. Stores, of course, should be made more accessible to older generations and should be made user-friendlier to seniors. Many manufacturers have realized that the boomers will become an ever more important segment of the market and have adjusted their product lines accordingly. For example, portions of foods in grocery stores are more geared to couples or singles in an attempt to satisfy a growing market niche.

When it comes to food, the older-aged shopper prefers the value and quantity of fast food like a teenager, but also enjoys the ambiance of a nice restaurant. As for entertainment, this is a demographic that is largely ignored. Movies especially are targeted to younger audiences, and this may be an area where the movie industry may be doing a disservice to itself.

The conundrum presented by the aging baby boomers for the retailer then is two-fold. As boomers get older they will have more time to shop but will suffer the double blow of being less interested in buying things and being more susceptible to sticker shock. The conclusion to be drawn from this scenario is that the shopping impact of the aged boomers will lessen as they get older. While this huge demographic group is still a shopping force to be reckoned with, it will start to have less and less effect on the retail market as it suffers the common experiences of aging. In spite of their own self-proclaimed importance, the significance of the boomers as a retail phenomenon will begin to diminish. It will fall into the hands of their heirs to spend their huge accumulated wealth.

Conclusion

From the perspective of the discussions above, shopping plays three roles. It defines the self, it defines the self to others, and it rewards the self. Thus shopping represents a complex behavior that serves a variety of purposes. It is not simple. Nevertheless, it is possible to understand a great deal about the demographics of shopping just by observing how various groups shop. What is clear is that marketers and retailers have to pay attention to the subtle characteristics of each demographic. Each group has the same basic justifications and motivations for shopping, but they also have particular needs and desires that should be understood and catered to.

Index

*For Product Safety Concerns and Information please contact
our EU representative GPSR@taylorandfrancis.com Taylor & Francis
Verlag GmbH, Kaufingerstraße 24, 80331 München, Germany*

T - #0150 - 270225 - C0 - 219/153/8 - PB - 9781138739314 - Gloss Lamination